Homeless at
HARVARD

JOHN CHRISTOPHER FRAME

Homeless at HARVARD

FINDING FAITH AND FRIENDSHIP ON THE STREETS OF HARVARD SQUARE

We want to hear from you. Please send your comments about this book to us in care of zreview@zondervan.com. Thank you.

ZONDERVAN

Homeless at Harvard
Copyright © 2013 by John Christopher Frame

This title is also available as a Zondervan ebook. Visit www.zondervan.com/ebooks.

This title is also available in a Zondervan audio edition. Visit www.zondervan.fm.

Requests for information should be addressed to:
Zondervan, *Grand Rapids, Michigan 49530*

Library of Congress Cataloging-in-Publication Data

Frame, John Christopher, 1978-
    Homeless at Harvard : finding faith and friendship on the streets of Harvard
Square / John Christopher Frame.
        pages cm
    ISBN 978-0-310-31867-5 (pbk.)
    1. Homeless persons—Massachusetts—Cambridge. 2. Harvard Square
(Cambridge, Mass.)—Social conditions. I. Title.
HV4506.M4   F73 2013
362.5'62092—dc23   2013001839

Published in association with literary agent Blair Jacobson of D.C. Jacobson & Associates LLC, an Author Management Company, www.dcjacobson.com.

The poem "Is Love Not Timeless?" written by Dane Alan Brun, is printed with his permission.

Cover design: Faceout Studio
Cover photography: Ayşegül Bektaş Frame

15 14 13 12 11 10 9 8 7 6 5 4 3 2 1

CONTENTS

NOTE TO THE READER

The names and identifying details of some people in this book have been changed. While this is a work of nonfiction and the author has selected what to include, it is based on his own perspective, notes, and recollection of events. The author thanks the real-life members of the Harvard Square homeless community portrayed here for accepting him during the times they shared together. The author especially thanks Neal, Dane, George, and Chubby John for sitting down with him and sharing their stories when he was writing this book. These interviews were conducted during the summer of 2012, three years after the author spent time on the streets of Harvard Square. The author's royalties from the sale of this book are being contributed to charities to help people in need.

Let us be dissatisfied until the tragic walls that separate the outer city of wealth and comfort and the inner city of poverty and despair shall be crushed by the battering rams of the forces of justice. Let us be dissatisfied until those that live on the outskirts of hope are brought into the metropolis of daily security. Let us be dissatisfied until slums are cast into the junk heaps of history, and every family is living in a sanitary home.

— **Martin Luther King Jr.**
"SCLC Presidential Address," August 16, 1967

INTRODUCTION

I stood and gawked. Bundled in warm blankets and sleeping bags, people were asleep and nestled under the outdoor alcove of the Harvard Coop bookstore, across the street and about a hundred feet away from the gates of Harvard Yard. They were motionless, like bodies ready to be picked up by an undertaker; lonely, like campers expelled from an expedition.

I had decided to get off the subway to look around a place that was as foreign to me as the homeless individuals now sleeping in my presence. I was sightseeing that October night while in Boston for a conference. However, I wasn't expecting to see anything, or rather *anyone*, like this in Harvard Square, the business district around Harvard University.

Leaving Harvard Square that night, I didn't know if I'd ever walk by that bookstore again. Soon, though, I'd meet some of the people who had slept there. And less than two years later, I was sleeping there myself.

That night was similar to a night a year earlier in London, England, when I met a homeless man who was sitting on a sidewalk next to a King Rooster fast-food chicken restaurant. I had walked by him twice, and then wrestled with a voice within me telling me to turn around, go back, and offer him one of the two bananas I had just purchased at the corner market. I gave in to it.

As I approached the man, he reached out his hand and said in a British accent, "Sir, could you do me a favor? Here's five pounds. Will you go in there and buy me a dinner?" As he dropped the coins in my palm, I noticed that his hand was cold and chapped, cracked and seeping blood.

This was my first experience of meeting a homeless person, and he was giving *me* money, entrusting me with perhaps all the money he had. I asked him what he would like. "Chicken dinner" was all he said, in a broken, almost stuttering voice. When I returned with his meal, we talked for a while on the sidewalk, his two-liter bottle of white cider beside him. We shared the same first name, and I learned that John had a debilitating muscular disease, a teenage son, and a mother he loved but had not seen in a long time.

John sat on the sidewalk and his cane rested against the restaurant. Passersby gave him coins, which he graciously accepted, and after a few minutes, a man and a woman joined us. John openly shared with us about his troubles. He cried as we prayed together, as if his brokenness — or maybe it was hopelessness — needed to be heard. Though I left John that night to return to the comforts of my privileges, our brief encounter stayed with me.

I grew up in a red brick house with a large, narrow lawn that my friends and I imagined as a major league baseball field. All summer long we played baseball with a yellow plastic bat and ball, trying to hit the ball over the fence into the church parking lot behind the parsonage where I lived. I announced every hit and strikeout as if I were broadcasting it like the radio voice of the Detroit Tigers, Ernie Harwell, and we dreamed of being as good as the players pictured on our bubblegum cards. Then we'd ride our bikes and play cops and robbers with my collection of cap guns and metal handcuffs, which looked as genuine as the ones in the police shows on TV. Because my dad was the pastor of a small church and my mom was a part-time teacher, my sister and I didn't grow up in a rich family. We had everything we needed, though, and most things any boy would hope to have, like a Nintendo, a cocker spaniel named Dixie who was my best friend, a newspaper route, and a fishing pole and a tackle box. Each night, I'd help set the table that my family gathered around for a homemade meal, and I was in our church several times each week. Besides seeing a few people around our city who looked down and out, I really knew nothing about homelessness.

In my late twenties, while pursuing a master's degree at Anderson University School of Theology, I felt inspired to get to know those who were living on the streets. My friends at Anderson, the author of a book I had read, and spring break trips to Atlanta to serve with a homeless ministry there helped me better understand how Christians should be concerned about the poor.

The day after I moved into my dorm on Harvard's campus in 2008 to begin a theology degree, I met a homeless man, George, sitting near his bedding, which was strewn out in front of a bank in Harvard Square. George helped me learn more about homelessness, as did some of his friends, such as Chubby John. I began spending time with them and also volunteering at the student-run Harvard Square Homeless Shelter, partly to fulfill a requirement for a Poverty Law class I was enrolled in. I began learning more about homelessness and about the relationships that help homeless people survive on the streets.

In a leadership class I took at Harvard, my professor taught us about translating life experiences into new actions that serve a greater purpose. I thought some more about how what I was learning about homelessness could be translated into something that could benefit others. For a long time, I'd wanted to write a book that could somehow make a difference, and I thought that by sharing my experiences with homeless people more broadly, I could help others think about building relationships with people on the streets. It seems that those who do not know homeless people are often unaware of their circumstances and struggles. In general, many of us are unaware of how the homeless view themselves and their difficulties. We're unaware of how similar we are to individuals who are panhandling on the sidewalk. A glimpse of the experiences of those who live on the streets could help change that, I thought.

The thought of temporarily staying on the streets with the homeless had begun to grow in my mind since my second spring-break trip to Atlanta. So while taking my final class at Harvard during the summer of 2009, I took the plunge and slept outside among the homeless community for ten weeks. I didn't do it as a way to emulate Christ or to show that living on the streets is more righteous than living in a home. And I didn't do it in an effort to save people on the streets from their homelessness. Rather, I hoped it would give me a chance to learn about homelessness as an insider, which would better enable me to write about the stories and struggles of those who were really homeless; and I could share what it was like to spend a summer on the streets.

This book is not a story about *me* as a homeless person, for I was never truly homeless. Rather, it's a story about a homeless community and how my life and the lives of those on the streets were woven together into a special tapestry.

For me, hanging out on the streets was only temporary. I did not give up one life to embrace another. I could not put aside the fact that I had a loving family, and that I was a student at Harvard Divinity School with access to Harvard buildings, books, and bathrooms that my homeless friends didn't have access to. But despite having privileges that my homeless friends didn't have, they accepted me, just like they accepted each other. The gap between us didn't seem to matter. The homeless community befriended me and shared with me some of the wisdom they'd gained from years of living in their culture.

The ten weeks I spent on the streets provided me with an experience I'd never had before. It gave me a chance to begin new friendships and to deepen relationships with people I already knew, such as Dane. Dane was a former cocaine addict and notorious criminal who'd had an epiphany after losing one of his toes, setting him in a new direction. However, he remained on the streets. Another was Neal, who had been sleeping outside for many years in Harvard Square. Over the summer, he and I talked about life and love, friendship and faith. Although he claimed to live a happy-go-lucky life, by the end of the summer, I learned about the health problems that he endured.

In this book, you're going to meet some of those friends, such as Neal, Dane, Chubby John, and George.

Welcome to the community of the homeless at Harvard.

In the words of GEORGE

I was pretty much buzzed that first night I met John. He was new to me. And you know how many students I used to see? I'd probably seen more than the professors in their classrooms throughout the year. We kept talking. Once I talk to somebody, I won't forget their name. I got to know John, and he was trying to figure out what it was like out here. I said, "Yeah, I'll show you the ropes, if you want to see them." But that was up to him to decide, not me. When he came out here for the summer, I was just wondering if he was going to turn around and say heck with school and be stuck on the streets like the rest of the people. Because I've seen that. The street will grab ya.

I was in junior high when I came down here to Harvard Square. We used to steal bikes. It was so easy to steal bikes and sell them. Back in them days, they didn't have bike racks; students just left their bikes out there when they went to class. Then I caught the second riot for the Vietnam War here in Harvard Square. We skipped school and were up in the Coop bookstore watching them. I think I was ten, maybe eleven.

I got involved with drinking and then drugs and all that, and getting in trouble here and there, and the family was getting upset. They hated me being on the street when they found out. I had a lot of runaway problems. They were always searching; I kept hiding. My family never threw me out. I just would get up and go. I'd get in an argument with my dad, and I hauled out of there. Nothing on my dad; it was just an excuse for me to get back out there and party with friends. My parents were good parents. My family's a good family. I was the only screwball out of the seven kids.

I got hooked up with some solid people on the street, and then the street grabbed me. That's just what happens. You're out there for a while and you get used to it, and the street ends up grabbing you. You don't realize it until it's too late. It was so comfortable being out there — everyone giving you everything.

On the streets, there's more freedom and less rules. I wanted to get off the streets quite a few times. It just didn't happen. I've had plenty of opportunities. I got jobs bartending and taking care of properties and stuff. But here comes the drugs again, and there goes the job. Thank God that I have no interest with drugs anymore. We were drinkers and pot smokers. I was smoking crack cocaine off and on for years. We did some drugs, but I didn't consider myself an addict. I could take it or leave it. But I considered myself an alcoholic. I haven't had drugs in years. And I haven't smoked pot in over a year and a half.

*I*f you're going to be homeless anywhere, Harvard Square is probably the best place to be. I know personally that there are services in Cambridge for the homeless, and there's no problem raising money. If you're hungry, you just tell somebody walking down the street and somebody's going to buy you a sandwich or pizza. I met many students just sitting on the street asking for money or asking for whatever I needed that particular day. I met many good ones out there.

For the homeless in general, I think everybody pretty much looks out for each other. You don't have to be a close friend with anybody, but they know who you are and you know who they are. You're all out there together. There are good and bad, like in all walks of life. You're going to meet homeless people who are out there who are well-educated, excellent people. Many of the homeless I met when I was out on the street in Harvard, I'm still friends with today. Many of them are now housed. Some of them are still on the street. I still visit with my friends over there, have a cup of coffee at the cafe and hang out.

I remember a good guy we knew out in the street named Jimmy.

Jimmy passed away, but he was the most generous, giving guy that you'd ever want to meet. When I first got my apartment, I was back in Harvard Square and I ran into him. And he said, "Sit with me and have a beer." The man didn't have a pot to pee in, and he told me, "You ever have any problems paying your rent, you come and see me. I'll run around through this traffic and get you every penny I can get." And while I was out on the street, a man who has no money and was collecting money in a cup used to put money in my cup, and I'd always tell him, "Why are you doing that?"

And he'd say, "Because it's the right thing to do. I made a little extra today, so I'll help you out."

And I'd say, "But you're going to need that a little later on, or tomorrow."

And he'd say, "Nah, it's alright; don't worry about it."

My first year of homelessness was down on the South Shore. I was staying in the woods in tents. I later stayed in a shelter in Harvard Square and got a job, putting money aside to work on getting housing without any assistance.

Then I had a heart attack, and everything changed.

Down on the South Shore, my old campsite wasn't the best. At the time, I thought that it was, though. But it was probably one of the worst. So I had hunted around the whole woods for a better place to camp. I found a better hidden spot, and I thought, *This is the spot*. You're not far from the subway. You're not far from the water fountain. Nobody's ever going to find you. Dog-walkers don't go over in that area. Nobody goes over in that area. It was the perfect spot in the world to go to.

Later on, when I needed a spot in the woods to stay again, that was where I was going back to. And I went there and set up camp. And then another friend of mine came and set up camp with me.

That was a nice little spot. Nobody ever found us. After I got my apartment, my friend from the South Shore stayed there for two years and nobody ever found him. And there were only four or five people who knew where that spot was.

To get there, you'd come down the road and there was this big tree. I made sure I had some landmark so I'd know how to get in there. Once you passed the tree, and you cut off to the right, there was a path. I cut the path out with a machete. I should have zig-zagged it a little more.

It could get pretty dark down there on some nights. When the cloud cover was low and heavy, and you had no moon or starlight to get in there, sometimes I had to use the little glow of my cell phone to find my way.

If you walked straight down the path and then went off to the left, there was a small tent where my friend stayed. Then there was a tent straight ahead where John stayed for his week out there. Then there was a tent over on the righthand side where I stayed. And we kind of had the middle area with a few chairs. I called it the living room in the middle. It was just a space to hang out.

one

THE CAMP AND THE COOP

Like harmless citizens unalarmed by the officer's presence, we calmly walked in front of the police cruiser, on the opposite side of the road, hoping the officer would ignore us. We walked as though we were out for a late-night stroll, not as though we were on our way to sleep in a nearby patch of woods. When the officer couldn't see us anymore, we crossed the street and successfully entered the pitch-black forest where Chubby John had made his home.

One of our friends had given Chubby John his name that summer, but I always just called him John. People never would have suspected he was homeless, unless they saw him shaking a cup on the sidewalk outside the twenty-four-hour CVS Pharmacy. The first time Chubby John accompanied me to an afternoon tea event on Harvard's campus, he had a conversation with an elderly man there and evaded every question about where he lived. "I sure wasn't gonna tell him I was homeless," he told me. "All the valuable things in that place? They woulda checked my pockets before I left."

From the first time I met Chubby John, he always reminded me of Hal, a fiftysomething man from the town I grew up in. John was younger than Hal, but like him, he always wore blue jeans and a hat and easily made friends with strangers. They were both opinionated and used their hands expressively as they talked, engaging me with their stories, which I could listen to for hours. Hal ate Milk-Bones sometimes and told me once he could poop in his living room with people standing around watching him. Chubby John said he had a plan to end homelessness forever if he could just convince the right elected officials to implement his idea.

I met Chubby John around the time I began volunteering at the Harvard Square Homeless Shelter. A few months after I met him, he did me a huge favor by meeting me at the hospital after I had minor surgery on my little finger. I felt a little humiliated when Chubby John saw me in the hospital bed. My blankets and hospital gown covered me, but I was still embarrassed, knowing that underneath the gown I was stark naked, as white as the sheets on the bed. My hand was bandaged with a dressing that looked like a boxing glove, as if I had been wounded in a fight.

A one-hour surgery on my finger didn't seem to warrant having to be escorted out of the hospital. Most guys would have asked their girlfriend or parents to pick them up. I didn't have a girlfriend, and my parents lived more than eight hundred miles away. So I asked Chubby John.

Chubby John had been homeless for three or four years, and ever since I'd known him, he'd been living in the woods or the Harvard Square Homeless Shelter in the basement of Harvard Square's University Lutheran Church. Chubby John had always seen me as a volunteer, as a student, and as someone who sometimes hung out on the sidewalk to chat. Now he was seeing me in a vulnerable situation, and he was my ticket to getting released. We walked out of the hospital into the cold February wind, and because Chubby John didn't have a car, we boarded the subway back to Harvard Square.

As we walked to his camp a few months later, Chubby John wasn't just someone I hung out with in my free time; he was my mentor. John had invited me to stay in one of his extra tents at his secret campsite after I expressed interest in spending the summer with the homeless.

John oriented me to the area, like a manager instructing a new employee. We had taken the subway pretty far south of Harvard Square to the South Shore, a few miles south of Boston. I mentally took notes so I could find my way to the campsite.

Walk through the Stop & Shop parking lot, toward the medical clinic. Walk through the bank's parking lot; turn right at the corner. Walk ten minutes past the Catholic church, and turn right at the high school.

As we walked, spotting the police cruiser parked about a hundred yards from where we needed to enter the woods, Chubby John told me, "The cops around here hate homeless people. You sure don't want to run into cops down here."

On Harvard's campus, the police were always friendly, but I had never taken the subway quite this far south. Apparently I had a lot to learn.

"If the police ever stop you, just give 'em your ID. Don't offer 'em any information," Chubby John warned me a couple of days later. "Only answer the questions they ask you. If they ask you where you're going, say 'up the street.' If they ask you where you live, say 'wherever I lay my head.'"

Even after hearing horror stories from Chubby John about the police, though, I didn't feel worried. I imagined that for me, an encounter with the police would involve showing the officer my Harvard ID and probably receiving a strange look and a "good day." To Chubby John, even thinking about the police may have reminded him of hiding while the police wandered through the woods with their German shepherd.

Once we reached the woods, I followed Chubby John down a winding path through large shrubs, weeds, and trees. For him, walking through the woods at midnight with only the light from the moon was something he did each night. I had to use the tiny built-in flashlight on my prepaid cell phone so I wouldn't stumble or get poked in the eye by a tree limb.

"The other night," Chubby John said quietly, "I was walkin' through here and some crazy animal came out tryin' to attack me." Reenacting the event with his shoulder bag, he said, "I took my bag and went *wham* and scared it away. I think it was a crazy coon or somethin'." Chubby John was always animated when he spoke. He had a Boston accent, and he talked something like the guys in the movie *Good Will Hunting*. And when he spoke, he almost never said "um" or "uh." It was like a special gift he had.

It took us only about one minute to walk down the path to the campsite. "Jim's sleeping over there," Chubby John said, pointing his flashlight toward a two-man tent that housed his friend. "And that one is yours," he said, pointing to a larger tent tucked into the brush and trees that was covered with a tarp weighed down by pools of water.

We stood in the middle of the camp — the "living room" — next to a pile of empty beer cans and three green fabric lawn chairs that Chubby John had found abandoned in Harvard Square. We talked in the dark of the night as if we were still on the sidewalk in front of the CVS Pharmacy in the middle of the afternoon.

"I want to get one of those screen tents and a grill and set it right here so I can cook out and not get wet or eaten up by mosquitoes," he said, motioning with his hands how and where he dreamed about developing the site. Some clothes hung over low tree limbs, soaked from the rain, with little possibility of drying out in the cold, wet June weather.

The woods were bordered by a paved road, a large field, and a salt marsh that receded with the daily ocean tides. On the other side of the marsh was a subdivision; its inhabitants were oblivious to our existence, as were the people who played sports on the field and drove by on the road. John was proud of finding this patch of woods.

I didn't enjoy being away from running water and a clean bed, but I was extremely grateful to John for the tent he had ready for me. Although I was mentally prepared to begin my summer among the homeless, I was not ready for a cold night in the woods. Actually, I was dreading it. I had left my sleeping bag, blanket, and sweatshirt in the divinity school library, unaware that it would close before my class ended that evening. I had on a button-down dress shirt and jeans — not exactly what you'd want to wear into the forest on a cold, rainy night.

"I've got an extra sleeping bag in my tent," Chubby John said. "I've never used it. Somebody gave it to me, and I've kept it just in case somebody needed it." I couldn't pass up his offer. Anything would be better than spending the night in a cold, wet tent without a sleeping bag in clothes that I didn't want to get dirty.

Chubby John crawled into his tent, and I peeked for the first time into the place he considered home. Though I knew he slept in the woods, I had no idea what this part of his life was really like. He used a reclining lawn chair topped with a warm sleeping bag as his bed. "See, I've got my radio and everything in here," he said as he reached for the extra sleeping bag, which was neatly rolled up.

I took the sleeping bag and wiggled my way past a few shrub twigs to the tent. I used the flashlight on my cell phone to look inside before crawling in, and noticed a large puddle of water just inside the door.

I untied the sleeping bag, which released an odor that apparently had been marinating for quite some time. As I laid the sleeping bag diagonally across the middle of the wet floor, I felt as though my hands were becoming dirty. I laid down on top of it, but there was no way I could bring myself to unzip it and crawl inside. I could feel a tree stump poking into my back and the ground sloping both sideways and down.

The temperature outside was dipping into the fifties, and it felt like my body temperature was not far behind. Taking my arms out of the sleeves of my T-shirt, I tucked them near my chest and used my long-sleeve shirt as a blanket and cover for my head. I looked like a guy strapped in a straitjacket who had just died. I took deep breaths, blowing into my shirt like a cold dragon, trying to keep warm. Each exhalation gave me about three seconds of reprieve, but no matter what I did, I was cold.

I'm going to have to get inside the sleeping bag, I thought in desperation. I hoped the inside of it wouldn't smell as bad as I'd imagined it might.

It did.

I unzipped the bag and sniffed inside. It was like sticking my nose into a pile of dirty laundry. I zipped the bag back up. *I'll just be cold,* I resolved.

I had thought a lot about being in the woods with Chubby John. I had envisioned a dry tent, but rainwater had made the entire floor wet. I had envisioned warm weather, but now I was fighting goose bumps. I had envisioned being happy as I nestled into my tent, but now I was discontent, like a vacationer who'd envisioned a trip to Maui but wound up in northern Siberia. And although we were tucked away in the woods, I knew that anybody or anything could come through the camp at any time.

I woke up the next morning to the voices of Chubby John and Jim, who were sitting in lawn chairs in their "living room," smoking cigarettes and drinking beer. I unzipped the tent, inconspicuously relieved myself in the woods, and emerged from the cavelike bushes.

"John, this is Jim," Chubby John said.

We shook hands and exchanged pleasantries. Jim was a burly man about fifty years old who had been homeless for twenty-five years; his most distinctive feature was a bushy gray moustache. He had been drinking and seemed in good spirits, even though he had woken in the middle of the night to walk to an agency to try to sign up at 4:30 a.m. for a day-labor job. Lately, though, the prospects of work were so grim that he and the other men looking for day-labor jobs were often turned away.

"How'd ya sleep?" Chubby John asked me.

"Not so well."

"Oh, it takes a couple nights to get used to the sounds of the woods," he assured me. I didn't want to tell John that I had been cold or that I couldn't bear the smell of the inside of the sleeping bag. Neither were his fault.

Jim handed me two strawberry granola bars. "The tent's a lot better than the cement, especially in the winter," he said. After my restless night's sleep, I couldn't imagine sleeping on cement, especially in the freezing cold.

I itched to get back to Harvard Square — the Square, as most of us called it. As we left, John commented, "It's good to have different people peeing in the woods, ya know. It keeps the coyotes away. They think there's a pack around here, and it scares them."

Maybe he was right. I wasn't going to argue. I was just glad that John was happy to have me there.

When you live on the streets, you eat as cheaply as you can. You take food from strangers who offer it. You go to the free weekly dinners at local churches. You wait in front of the Upper Crust Pizzeria after 11:00 p.m. hoping for leftovers when they close. You take promotional items, like free Vitaminwater, being passed out on sunny days by companies marketing their products in busy Harvard Square, a hub for smart, bourgeois young people. I even filled out surveys and did a little test for psychology students that netted me a piece of candy for my participation. And each week there were street ministries providing food to people on the streets. There was a saying among the homeless community that if you're homeless in Harvard Square and you starve to death, it's your own fault.

Most of the people I knew on the streets, some of whom received benefits from the government, would have gone hungry before eating out of the dumpster. Andy, however, often scavenged in trash bins in hopes of finding scraps of leftovers tossed by patrons of the many yuppie restaurants that filled the Square. We all felt sorry for him. Andy would mumble to himself as he walked around and sometimes waved his hands erratically, as if he were fighting off a ghost only he could see. Most of the time, his facial expression was caught between sadness and pain, as though someone had been scolding him all of his life.

Andy was unlike anyone else in the homeless community; in

fact, he wasn't really a part of it. He lived in his own world and didn't talk to anyone. When I said hi to Andy, sometimes he returned the greeting, but often he just ignored me.

Andy slept outside of a storefront where, every night at around nine thirty, he created a lean-to shelter out of a twenty-by-twenty-foot tarp. Then every morning before the store opened at nine, he took his tarp down and locked it in a secret location he had arranged with the shop. This was his daily ritual. It seemed to me that his days consisted of waiting for the store to close at night so he could stretch out the tarp and recreate his living area, a quiet spot just for him that was safe and comfortable.

One morning, Neal, one of my constant companions, and known in the Square for his jovial personality, gave me a carryout box with a pita and hummus concoction that he had received from a stranger the night before. I ate a good part of it — pretty unappetizing fare for breakfast — and carefully set the remainder in a trash bin thinking that Andy would walk over to our block in Harvard Square and find it. Sure enough, Andy wandered over and ate my leftovers for breakfast.

Jared, a thirty-seven-year-old homeless vegan who bought high-end vegetables at Whole Foods with food stamps, closely watched Andy as he picked up the container I had set inside the trash bin. Jared was quick-witted and carried on a nonstop comedy routine. He was like a Harvard Square version of radio personality Howard Stern. Like a school bully always ready to pounce on the class nerd, he spouted, "I hate it when homeless people eat food out of our dumpster. His isn't dirty enough. There's no puke or dirt in his dumpster, so he has to come over to ours. Cause he likes to eat out of the dirtiest trash cans, with puke and mold and crap." Andy acted as though he hadn't heard Jared. Maybe in Andy's world, he hadn't.

Eating out of the trash didn't bother me, per se, for I had enjoyed the benefits of dumpster-diving long before my summer on the streets. You never know what prizes you might find, including unopened boxes of doughnuts, cakes, and other sweet treasures. Success lies in finding the *right* dumpster, although some of these locations where the dumpsters can be found — dark parking lots and foreboding warehouses — often look like crime scenes straight out of *Law & Order*.

I was particularly fond of Hostess snack cakes, and I found the perfect location to grab some for me and my friends on the streets. One night, I collected around twenty unopened boxes of snack cakes that would soon be on their way to a landfill. Dumpster-diving wasn't just a late-night free-food frenzy; it was saving food from its unfortunate destiny.

I stashed the doughnuts, Ho Hos, Ding Dongs, chocolate-chip minimuffins, and low-calorie cinnamon-streusel coffee cakes in a garbage bag in the shrubs around the parking lot of the subway station near Chubby John's campsite. The next day, because redemption is always worth celebrating and sharing, and as a way to extend a token of friendship to those on the streets, I distributed some of the goodies among the homeless community, handing out the boxes of treats from the garbage bag as if they were gifts at Christmas.

After a week in the woods at Chubby John's camp, I decided to begin sleeping in Harvard Square. At fifteen dollars a week, my subway pass to get to the tent in the woods was a cost I didn't wish to bear. And I wanted to begin sleeping in Harvard Square, since that's where I had chosen to be for the summer.

I decided to begin sleeping under the outdoor alcove of the

Harvard Coop bookstore, the same place I had stood less than two years before, gazing at the people asleep there. The Coop (pronounced "coop" and not "co-op") was Neal's regular sleeping spot and seemed to me the best place to better acquaint myself with the homeless community. I learned later that only the brave — or the really desperate — slept there.

"No, you ain't gonna sleep in the Coop," George said to me, like a principal instructing a deviant child. "You'll stay with me on the porch of the Red Doors Church, or we can sleep right here," he said, pointing to the Cambridge Common, a large park in town, where we were standing and where other homeless people slept.

George was the first homeless person I had met in Harvard Square, when I had seen his blankets on the sidewalk, the day after I moved to Cambridge. I paused to read his cardboard sign, near a bowl with a few coins in it. George called out to me from across the sidewalk, where he was sitting with a couple of friends; he had one of the strongest Boston accents I'd ever heard. He politely extended his hand to shake mine. His hands looked something like my mother's hands, crooked and deformed from rheumatoid arthritis. He wore on his right ring finger an Irish heart ring positioned with the heart outward, a subtle sign that George, like the rest of us, desired love.

I felt as though I was supposed to befriend George. One time, I invited him to join me for lunch in a Harvard dining hall, but he politely declined, mentioning that he didn't feel comfortable going inside. Instead, I brought a sandwich for him to the bench he was sitting on in front of the CVS Pharmacy, where the homeless often gathered in Harvard Square.

George was instrumental in helping me learn about homelessness. The things that he said and did helped me understand the world he lived in. George knew I was interested in learning about homelessness and had told me, "I'll help you however I can, John. You just let me know."

George was someone I felt I could trust. And George didn't want me to get hurt while I spent the summer on the streets. I assured him that I would be safe sleeping under the alcove of the Coop and that Neal would be sleeping close by.

The day before I began sleeping there, people told me horror stories about what could happen. I could get head and body lice, beaten up, robbed, or urinated on. Jared told a story about a woman peeing in her covers and then trying to get into his. And somebody else smiled and said, "Be sure you don't sleep downstream!"

Chubby John had vowed never to sleep in the Coop, but Neal had said he slept there because it was convenient and legal. Neal also said, "I love being homeless," bursting out with a big laugh, his raspy vocal cords shuddering with each exhalation. "I don't have to pay rent. I get free rent right here," he said, as he pointed to the floor tiles in the Coop's alcove. "I can put all my money in my pocket." Neal's comments were similar to what George once told me when I asked if he liked being out in Harvard Square: "I do, but I don't."

Underneath Neal's laughter and humor, though, was a man who wished to get off the streets. He dreamed of someday getting a small apartment with a friend of his.

"But if I did win the Powerball," he said, sitting down on the tiles, "I'd buy a farm on about twenty acres in Vermont. I'd have a house built and buy a nice car." I'm not sure how often Neal bought a Powerball ticket, but it wasn't a habit. Usually he just bought tickets out of boredom, and usually they were scratch-off tickets, rather than tickets that won if the numbers matched the daily pick. "I'm bored, John," he'd say. "I think I'll buy a scratch ticket." Then he'd walk into the liquor store near CVS, buy one scratch ticket, bring it outside, and scratch the gray coating off with his thumbnail. If he won, he'd ponder whether he should take it back inside and buy another. If he didn't win, he'd say, "Oh, well," and toss it into the air as if he really didn't care. Neal told me that buying them was like "taking money and throwing it into the toilet."

Whereas security guards chased homeless people out of bank buildings that had twenty-four-hour ATM access, and police might make people sleeping in other parts of the Square move on, at the time the police didn't have a problem with people sleeping in the Coop. Still, each night, Neal mulled over where to sleep, as if it were the day's great decision. For Neal, the safety of his large cart, and the burden of wheeling it to his sleeping spot, was something he considered before deciding where to bed down. Sometimes he considered sleeping in front of a nearby bank. "I know everyone who works in there, and they don't care if I sleep here," he'd say. But that would have been risky. The police or a security guard might wake him up and make him leave. Sometimes Neal would sleep on "Neal's Island," the place everyone else knew as the bus stop. Neal spent a lot of his time there. He said that he had things stolen in the past while he slept in the Coop, such as his DVD player, but he also told me that detectives watched out for people who slept there. At least that's what he believed. He told me the police had arrested someone once who was rifling through his stuff. The police woke up Neal and asked him if he knew the perpetrator. When Neal said he didn't know him, they hauled the suspect off to jail.

Neal also said that sometimes he woke up and found five- or ten-dollar bills or food lying beside him from Good Samaritans who passed by during the night. I hoped that I would be surprised like that too.

After Neal went to sleep and Chubby John left for his tent in the woods, I walked by the Coop, strategizing about where I could lay down when I was ready to settle in for the night.

At 1:00 a.m. I finally chose my spot, right next to where Neal was sleeping. I took my little blanket and carefully folded it to make a one-foot-wide cushion, then laid my sleeping bag down on top of it. If I didn't move much in the night, I would stay pretty comfortable on my makeshift mattress. There were six other people scattered under the alcove, which was a space about twenty feet by twenty feet.

I took off my shoes and, because I don't like to be dirty, made sure that I didn't step on the tiles with my socks. Then I positioned my backpack as my pillow, and in what became my normal practice, I stuck the ends of my shoes under my backpack, so if someone wanted an old pair of Asics, my head would be jostled during the attempted theft and I would wake up. It wasn't that my shoes were valuable; it's just that they were my only pair.

Then I laid down and tried to sleep. I pulled the sleeping bag over my head and covered my face to provide whatever privacy was possible. I had rarely felt so on display. Passersby all night long and into the morning would see me sleeping there. With my bright-red fleece sleeping bag, I was sure to be the first one they'd notice.

Pigeons cooed and ruffled their feathers as they nested on top of the store display cases lining both sides of the Coop's alcove. Sometimes the pigeons flew from one display case to the next, as if they were suffering insomnia or having domestic problems. But they were not nearly as loud as the pedestrian signal a few feet away on the street. Every time the traffic light changed, twelve loud chirping sounds pierced the air like an electronic cuckoo clock, alerting pedestrians that they could safely cross the road. Every few minutes, a bus drove by, and I'm quite certain that every bus driver gunned the engine as it rounded the corner by the Coop, the thunder echoing in the alcove.

A man stumbled in and out of our sleeping area a few times, mumbling incoherently. And another guy who always wore a Red Sox shirt — who was always drunk and slept in the Coop without any blankets or a sleeping bag, even when it was cold — came in and made some noise before he went to sleep, though he was very apologetic when he thought he'd disturbed me.

About forty-five minutes after I laid down, a city public works crew began power-washing the brick sidewalk, using hoses to whisk away litter and grime with powerful jets of water from a machine that sounded like an idling lawn mower.

When you sleep outside, you have to be ready for interruptions, knowing that, whether it is because of weather conditions or people disturbing your peace to do midnight cleaning, sleeping outside is no Holiday Inn.

A few days later, I heard a group of people walk by the Coop commenting about "the homeless," as if their own circumstances couldn't change, landing them there themselves someday. At 4:40 that same night, a man yelled, "Anybody want some pizza?" Seeing me squirm in my sleeping bag to peek out, he asked, "Hey, man, you want some pizza?" as though he were passing out hundred-dollar bills. "It's cold, but here you go." I decided to take a slice, but I would have preferred not to be awakened. He then woke another man, who politely responded, "No, thanks."

That first night in the Coop, I huddled in my sleeping bag, hoping I'd fall asleep soon. At 2:00 a.m., a tall woman wearing a gray miniskirt and a brown sweater and carrying two bags sat down between Neal and me.

The closeness of her face startled me as I peeked out from my cocoon. I said a polite hey as if it were nothing abnormal to have a stranger crowding my personal space while I was trying to go to sleep. I had seen her earlier that evening panhandling by CVS, holding a picture of herself as a child with Santa Claus. Her name was Teresa, and she was new to Harvard Square.

Teresa tried to get Neal's attention. But he was sound asleep. "David didn't open the door for me tonight," she said in a heartbroken tone. Neal didn't budge. "David didn't open the door for me tonight," she said again.

"Lie down right here," Neal said, patting his hand on the tiles between us.

She sat on his sleeping bag, looking confused and alone. She blew her nose and cried. Her legs were bare, and I imagined she was cold.

I lay there considering what to do. I thought about opening up my sleeping bag so she would have a place to lay down. After a few minutes, I sat up and unzipped my bag. Without giving her a chance to say no, I said, "Teresa, you can use my sleeping bag; I'm going to go up the street. I can't sleep." And then I picked up my backpack, put on my shoes, and left, hoping to get my sleeping bag back the next morning.

I found a couple of homeless people I knew sitting next to the bank. One of them was Bernard, who was mostly nocturnal. After a few minutes, the two of us walked to a couple of benches where he planned to try to stay warm for the night. Bernard snuggled with his sleeping bag while we sat on the bench, which was wet from an earlier rain. "You shouldn't give your stuff away," he scolded in his typically terse manner. "You need that."

I soon made my way to the Red Doors Church — a church in town that all the homeless identified by the color of its doors —

where I thought I would be able to get some sleep on its cement porch. Before I walked there, I passed by the Coop again and saw Teresa nestled comfortably in my sleeping bag next to Neal.

In the morning, Neal and Teresa were sitting together, trying to stay warm. "See my new girlfriend?" he asked, half-jokingly. She followed Neal around the rest of the day, giving him the attention he always loved, but denying she was his girlfriend. Neal seemed to like having Teresa as a new companion. Before the end of the summer, though, she would be gone, and we would all learn something about her that came as a big surprise.

Two

COPPER COINS AND A WOODEN CROSS

Have patience, my son! Pride is a sin," Neal hollered to me from Neal's Island as I stood along the side of the road clutching my empty red plastic cup.

Panhandling wasn't turning out to be very prosperous for me. Despite my blue jeans, dirty inside-out white T-shirt, and shaggy locks, I was sure I looked out of place. And indeed I was. A few minutes earlier, Neal had pranced down the road showing me how to panhandle to drivers who were conveniently stopped at the traffic light.

"Come on out here and try it, John," Neal had called. I finally had mustered up the courage and joined him, assuring myself that most of my friends at Harvard didn't have cars and that the likelihood of one of my professors driving by was slim.

You wouldn't think that panhandling — or stemming, as they called it — would be so nerve-racking. But I was jittery. Neal was a natural, making money simply by passing time. He moved to the beat of Beatles music playing in his earphones as if he didn't have a care in the world. I moved because I couldn't stand still.

Shaking my plastic cup back and forth, I stoically asked, "Got any spare change?" to drivers stopped at the red light. Some people awkwardly said hi, and one man told me he had just given away all of his change. But many of the drivers looked straight ahead. They had their windows rolled down, enjoying the evening breeze.

Our homeless friend Dane coached me from the curb and then came over to where I stood. "I think I look too clean-cut," I told him, certain that everyone passing by could see the invisible "Harvard Student" sign above my head.

"Oh, no, trust me, you look pretty unkempt compared to how you used to look," Dane assured me, noting that I looked every bit of the six days I had spent in the Square. "I think you should try a friendlier approach. What you're saying sounds a bit too rough," he said, referring to my blunt, "Got any spare change?" "How about trying, 'Could you help out with a little spare change?'"

I had to admit that did sound much nicer. And I liked how Dane said it. It was as if he were wishing people a happy birthday rather than asking them for money. If I could say it like Dane, surely every driver would say to me, "I'd love to help, buddy. How about a ten-dollar bill?"

Stemming became a little easier with each car that came by, but my plastic cup remained empty. I shook it as though I had collected a small quantity of coins that other drivers might feel they'd like to add to. But even though my stress decreased with every passing minute, I kept retreating from the traffic back to Neal and Dane, and they kept encouraging me to return.

"There's money getting away," Dane prodded.

"Practice makes perfect," I responded uneasily, returning to the side of the road.

Soon, a driver looked my way and nodded. I skittered over to his new, foreign-made sedan and spotted a large collection of dimes, quarters, and nickels in the center console. Instead of reaching into this glittering mine of silver, he reached into a coffee cup that probably kept things like paper clips and rubber bands. He dropped ten pennies into my cup, and I thanked him for his contribution. Although I was disappointed, he didn't have to give me anything. I was beginning to understand the difficulties of those who stemmed for money.

A couple of minutes later, a taxi driver reached out of his window and gave me two quarters. Elated, I smiled at Neal and Dane.

"When a taxi driver gives you money," Dane said, "tell him, 'I wish you good jobs and good tips.' He gave you money believing it will help him get better tips."

I had thought the driver had just given me the money out of the goodness of his heart, but Dane was the one who'd spent twenty-seven years driving a taxi in Boston.

Nobody likes panhandling. People don't like to be asked for money, and the homeless don't like asking for it. When you panhandle, you learn to remove yourself from the task you're performing. You come to ignore ridicule and feeling that you're an invisible man. It is a burden, but one you must bear in order to subsist. You accept it as a way of life. You accept it as part of being in need. Fortunately, I ultimately wasn't in need.

The plastic cup I held couldn't measure up to Neal's red, antique stained-glass bowl that fit so perfectly in the palms of his hands and reminded me of an old church window. Neal had acquired it from who knows where—one of many prized possessions in his hundred-pound metal cart, a treasure trove of intricately made wooden boxes, toys, an autoharp, and many other things, along with an extra forty-ounce bottle of beer.

"Let me see if there's any money out there," Dane declared. He got up from the park bench, picked up his cardboard sign, and walked confidently to where I had been stemming. He had netted forty dollars earlier at that spot. But after a few minutes, he had no luck and returned. *At least it wasn't just me,* I thought.

Then Neal tried again, while advising me how to master the art. It seemed he had a way of dazzling drivers just by dancing to music he listened to in his earphones. He even strutted along the side of the road with a special confidence. It was like he was onstage. "He's a seasoned, grizzled specimen, a real professional. He's direct, slow, assertive, docile," Dane commented in his characteristically erudite way of speaking that could fool anybody into thinking he was a Harvard professor.

Neal's clothes didn't look overly used or dirty, yet Neal *looked* homeless. And although I may not have looked like a typical Harvard student — whatever that looked like — I certainly was no Neal, prancing up and down the street singing "Here Comes the Sun," making drivers laugh as if he were the best show in town.

I didn't have Neal's years of experience panhandling in traffic. I wasn't animated. I didn't possess the carefree attitude that often netted him pocket money. "I made $2.70 in ten minutes!" Neal had boasted just a few minutes before I had tried my hand at stemming. However, although he had been certain he would be successful, this time he didn't get anything either. "Must be too late in the evening," he conceded.

There never was a good reason stemming worked sometimes and not other times. Chubby John had recently reported making

$1.25 after a few hours stemming in front of CVS. Then a stranger came by, set a bag of coins in front of him, and said, "Have a nice day." Chubby John fished eight gold dollars out of the bag as if they were his prize catch of the day, bought cigarettes, and took the rest of the coins to a change machine. He brought back sixty dollars. Success required persistence, patience, and a whole lot of luck — three things I didn't possess when it came to stemming.

Although my first panhandling experience lasted only a few minutes and mostly consisted of retreating in embarrassment to Neal's Island, I worried about how difficult it would be to sustain myself by stemming, and how much I would hate that. I soon realized that I didn't need to, or want to.

"John, you look stressed," Dane said.

"This isn't easy. It's hard out there," I said. "I was thinking about how hard it will be to make enough money to live."

Dane strummed his guitar and hummed a few tunes, undeterred by my lack of success. "You're stressed like you think you've got to be doing something. You should enjoy the various aspects of homelessness, like sitting back, being with friends, staying warm and dry."

Neal piped in, "Yeah, John, you've got to enjoy life." He considered himself a man of leisure and had years of experience living in Harvard Square in the warm months, and in warmer climates in the cold months. And Dane was speaking as one who'd served time in prison, and who'd been addicted to drugs for decades. Simply staying warm and dry was far better for him than many of his previous experiences.

Their words comforted me. I was stressed over failing at a very brief attempt at something I didn't even have to do. Actually, I wished that I had decided, before the summer began, to stay on the streets without feeling like I needed to panhandle or appear that I was part of the homeless community myself.

Some people on the streets knew me as a student before the summer began, and the homeless people I spent most of my time with that summer learned my story, if they didn't know it already. Yet I wish I had thought out how to better disclose my true identity to those who did not know me. I sometimes struggled with that.

Understanding my identity on the streets was a process in and of itself. For a while, I wrongly thought of myself as a homeless student, because I was spending time on the streets and didn't have an apartment. In fact, my only home was several states away. But I soon learned that homelessness entails more than not having a place indoors to lay your head. My original idea of attempting to be temporarily homeless was based on my desire to have the opportunity to write about the experience. I hoped it could help people better understand the struggles, experiences, and street life of the homeless. I now understand that that attempt was unnecessary and something that centered more on me, rather than on the men and women on the streets who knew what homelessness truly was. My friends on the streets were homeless. I wasn't.

An email correspondence that summer with a professor I'd later work with helped me better understand my place in the homeless community and feel more comfortable with my identity as a non-homeless student who was voluntarily spending time among the homeless. I learned that just because I slept outside didn't make me homeless. Similarly, just because someone sleeps inside doesn't make that person *not* homeless.

Now I could give lots of reasons why I didn't panhandle much over the summer, including the fact that I wasn't legitimately homeless, although there were some non-homeless people who did panhandle in the Square. Even though I didn't have a job, I had my own money that I was happy to live on. Plus I didn't want to waste time shaking a cup by myself when I could have been doing something else a little more productive, including sharing time with my homeless friends. The main thing I learned from panhandling with Neal and Dane that night was simple: I was scared to do it — or maybe too embarrassed. Whatever it was, I never panhandled in traffic again.

One night, about three months before I began staying on the streets, I watched Dane pull a cart loaded with clothes, food, and an electric guitar near the subway station in Harvard Square. The weather was cold, and I was volunteering on my shift at the Harvard Square Homeless Shelter. Our small team took the provisions of the shelter to people on the streets during our Wednesday evening shift. Six nights a week, during the months when the shelter was open, Street Team members stuffed blue and purple backpacks with gloves, scarves, sandwiches, fruit cups, and hot leftover Harvard food to give away to homeless people who did not stay in the shelter.

Dane wore decorative chains around his neck, one with an ankh cross and another with a gold Hindu symbol. He decorated his wrists with a collection of bracelets, and some of his fingers had a ring, including some simple black bands. An earring dangled from his left ear, complementing his nicely trimmed white beard and clean, short white hair. Like Neal, Dane sometimes wore patchouli cologne.

Dane was good at telling stories and was especially good at reciting his original poems. He had written a series of poems for a nurse he had once fallen for, though she was half his age. Beaming at his memory of her, he told me once, "She had big, gorgeous brown eyes that just sparkled like diamonds when she smiled. If she looked at me with more than a glance with those piercing eyes, it would just start to turn my insides to Jell-O and melt my heart like butter."

That night, he asked my Street Team friends and me, "Would you like to hear a poem I wrote about her?" He looked us in the eyes, grinned widely, and recited "Is Love Not Timeless?" with such emotion that the veins in his neck popped out:

> If I could only rearrange the pages of time
> I would no longer be so much older than her
> Nor she much younger than I.
> Yes, and a far more likely suitor I would then be
> While attempting to capture her eye.
> At that time I'm certain her heart I could win
> Once given my second try.
> For what in this world would I not give to only enjoy her
>   attention turned towards me?
> That I might see reflected in her eyes
> Just a flicker of the flame burning brightly in my heart for
>   only she.

Dane shared three poems with us that night on the sidewalk, along with a fair share of philosophy. Dane liked to talk to people and loved being onstage, and though he had only a fourth-grade education, he used words such as *ostentatious*, *formidable*, and *obstinate*. I always thought that Dane's education exceeded mine in a lot of ways.

"My mom taught me how to lie to bill collectors at the door," Dane told me once. "My mom cheated on my dad when he was gone to work. He'd come home and we'd be playing checkers and I couldn't tell him where Mom was. There were fifteen of us kids. I was the oldest. And some of the kids didn't look like my dad. They looked like the guy in the white Cadillac. When I was nineteen years old, all my top teeth had to be pulled because my mom didn't teach me how to brush my teeth. Same with my brothers and sisters."

Dane persevered through his adversity and, as a child, began reading books that his mother bought from a door-to-door salesman. He read the encyclopedia and all of the classics — *The Last of the Mohicans* was his favorite — and he looked up every word he didn't know in a dictionary that he kept beside him. Dane was a critical thinker, and while he was able to diversify his speech with street slang if he needed to, he was like a walking Webster's dictionary. He told me about the time when, as a cab driver, he and his passenger talked theology, philosophy, and spirituality all the way from the airport to the Copley Square Hotel. "While he was paying me through the window," Dane told me, "he said to me, 'At what university did you receive your doctorate, sir?'" When Dane told him he'd never graduated grade school, the man said, "I am a professor at Yale, and you sure fooled me."

But underneath the exterior, it seemed Dane's life was a patchwork of struggle and hardship. He had overcome a cocaine addiction only one year before I'd met him. He was once married and had fathered a couple of children, and I sensed that Dane suffered from both lost love and love unrequited. It seemed his soul may have been burdened, like a lost bird looking for its nest. He never said so, but I think Dane was lonely.

Dane didn't drink alcohol regularly because he liked to be articulate, and booze messed that up, he said. And he'd given up cigarettes thirty-six years earlier because they had affected his singing voice.

Proudly showing me his new silver ring and a couple of necklaces he had purchased from selling small quantities of marijuana, he said, "I can buy little things with the profits." He told me once, "One time I bought a bag for fifty dollars. Then a guy called me and wanted a hundred-dollar bag. I told him I'd be right there. I met him and he laid down five twenty-dollar bills and looked at what I had just bought and said, 'Wow, a nice fat bag!' He paid me a hundred dollars on his own volition and was a happy customer. In just a few minutes, I had doubled my money."

I knew Dane sometimes took things without paying for them. He preferred not to think of it as stealing, though. He talked about "nicking" batteries from a local store, then, justifying the theft, said, "At least I'm not stealing them from someone like when I did cocaine." Another time he said that hands were good for grabbing things. We all knew what he meant.

Although Dane sometimes clashed with others, he was generous when he had plenty. One night, Dane came to us on Neal's Island with three bags stuffed with large Subway sandwiches. A woman had bought them, and when her friends didn't show, she thought Dane might be able to put them to good use. "I'll share them with my kind," he happily told the stranger. We divided them among ourselves like thieves splitting loot from a break-in. I ate a meatball sub and took a tuna sub for Chubby John. Dane's good fortune that night made all of us very happy that we were his friends.

Neal was a man of faith, and very much aware of his alcoholism. At the time, Neal drank malt liquor from forty-ounce brown glass bottles. I once heard him say, "Even though I am an alcoholic and drink too much beer, and get angry and say things I shouldn't, I am a devout Christian," noting that he had to ask forgiveness from Christ when he believed he acted wrongly.

Neal was a sensitive man, and his gentleness belied his stature — six foot three, I believe. He was goofy, a self-proclaimed authority on New England birds, and, as if that weren't enough, a people-ologist — yes, one who studies people. And he'd been cultivating the art, off and on, for years in Harvard Square and other places around the country.

He had a full head of gray hair, usually topped with a red ball cap that said "Fire Safety Monitor," a gray mustache, a long, oval face, and bluish-green eyes. He often wore a loose-fitting, sky-blue button-down shirt, dark jeans, slip-on shoes, and an assortment of silver jewelry around his neck. Because he was able to display his fun side, people liked looking at him as much as he liked looking at them.

Chubby John called Neal a collector of junk because Neal had a little bit of everything in the cart he wheeled around. Neal admitted that hauling around his stuff was a burden. He once showed me from his cart an old quarter, a wax and seal set, a vase, and what he believed to be an uncut diamond.

One day, after a doctor's visit, Neal found an antique rocking chair. The bus driver wouldn't let him on the bus with it, so he hid it in a thicket of bushes next to a wall by Cambridge Hospital. He retrieved it a couple of days later, brought it to Harvard Square, began cleaning it up, and had visions of chaining it to a park bench and putting a sign on it: "Neal's Chair." His dream was dashed, though, when it went missing after he stashed it behind the brick wall of the Old Cambridge Burying Ground, the cemetery in Harvard Square.

People seemed to be naturally drawn to Neal, and among those he spent time with was Jared. Sometimes Jared would come by and ask me, "Where's Neal?" if Neal had gone missing for a little while. I think their friendship helped sustain their lives on the streets. Neal told me one time, "I love when Jared is around me. He's brilliant. I respect him. You lend him money, he pays you back."

Jared was sardonic, often referring to the homeless community as the "Millionaire's Ring." He sported a crew cut that he dyed bleach-blonde, and he had a voice that was always on full throttle. He'd make comments about how he hated homeless people, how he'd like to see an incinerator built for them in Cambridge Common, and how they could be lured there with free sandwiches.

One day Jared had a scuffle with a guy named Ricky, who came to Harvard Square sometimes to stem. Ricky often stemmed in traffic where I had tried my hand at it, and was said to be a drug user. Ricky was a little aggressive in his panhandling, usually because he needed another fix, according to others. On the day of their little brawl, Jared had left his stemming spot to use the restroom at the Red Doors Church, and Ricky jumped in and took his spot.

"Somebody came up to me and gave me a dollar for beating up Ricky," Jared later told Neal and me. "Everybody was watching it. We could have sold tickets," he said. Jared's version of the story included how a bus driver got involved trying to break up the fight. Neal said it lasted a half-hour, but that they weren't hurting each other, just scuffling.

Jared was never short on words, and at first I was so shocked by the vulgarity of what he said that I had to pretend to ignore him. He often ignored me anyway.

Neal told me it took him three years to get used to Jared. "That's why God invented headphones — for people like him," Neal said jokingly. "But we can still love him." Laughing at some of Jared's wit, Neal told me, "He'll say things to get a reaction out of you. But he only says the things he does because he's a shock jock. He should be on the radio — he'd make millions — or do stand-up comedy. He says things to shock you. But he really doesn't feel that way. You see, this whole area is his stage. When he comes out here, he's onstage."

Sometimes Harvard Square didn't seem big enough for all of its actors. Most of us didn't seek to be the object of everyone's attention, but fortunately Neal, Dane, and Jared were never shy about stepping front and center for our entertainment.

When I was a teenager, every Saturday morning I went to a farmers' market in an old freight house that sat along the railroad tracks in the town in which I grew up. At one end of the freight house was a little cafe, which was warmed by a wood-burning stove. The cafe had tables decorated with country tablecloths and an assortment of old plastic-covered padded chairs that looked as if a thousand people had sat in them before I was even born. I gathered with my friends, all of whom were at least forty years older than I was, and we chitchatted while the winter winds blew outside and the windows frosted up. Hours went by as we listened to live bluegrass and classic country music. After I learned how to play the spoons, the musicians asked me to join them on fast hillbilly songs like "The Wreck of the Old 97." It was the place to shake and howdy, to see and be seen.

For the homeless community in Harvard Square, the sidewalk outside of CVS was kind of like that old freight house. It didn't have music or a cafe or a wood-burning stove, but it did have lots of people who had plenty to talk about. It was also the place where new homeless people turned up and old ones returned after time away. It was our hub.

There was a mere twenty feet between the front of the store and the row of taxis that lined the curb on Massachusetts Avenue. But there was always plenty of room, despite the hundreds — maybe thousands — of tourists and students that walked by on the brick sidewalk every hour.

All of the park benches in front of CVS, except the one that a couple of guys had unscrewed from the sidewalk and turned toward the store years before, faced the taxis on the street. They were our lounge furniture, and the row of taxis coming and going and Harvard's palatial brick buildings and iron gates across the street were our decor. Huge wire baskets attached to lamp poles, filled with draping flowers, hung high above our heads, so high you never noticed them unless you looked toward the sky. A two-foot-high brick column protruded from the sidewalk, and we used it as a seat. A small honey locust tree near the street added to the scenery, but was too small to provide any significant shade.

It was the ideal place for people to meet and greet, find friends, and people-watch. Neal always said that people-watching in Harvard Square was better than watching television. One time, for example, before the summer, some of us watched undercover cops arrest a young woman who went berserk when they put handcuffs on her. She beat her head against the outside of the police car and nearly busted out the window when they finally got her inside.

It was here, outside CVS, that Neal would talk about the ridiculousness of Harvard Square. It was here that Neal would dance early in the morning to music on his portable CD player and say hi to attractive women walking by as if they were crossing his stage, interrupting his performance. It was here that we refreshed ourselves on hot days with tall cans of iced tea that we got on sale from CVS for fifty cents, and where we gathered at 11:30 at night to eat free leftover gourmet pizza from the Upper Crust Pizzeria — giant slices you had to use two hands to handle and that sometimes had artichokes on them.

I had been on the streets only a few days when Neal asked me there in front of the CVS, "When are you going to become one of us — all the way?"

"How do you do that?" I asked.

"You give up your job."

"I don't have a job," I said.

"Oh, okay," he responded, as though I were well on my way. He added, "You need to praise God every day you have life."

"Well, I think I do that," I said. Neal grinned widely as if he was welcoming me into his club.

I was surprised at such an off-the-wall question, especially from someone whom I had known for only a short time and who already knew I was a student. But through that brief exchange, I learned a lot about Neal and later cherished that he wanted me to be part of the homeless community "all the way" and to be his "one of us" friends.

Neal and I walked four minutes from CVS to Neal's Island, which looked like a giant patio, triangular in shape and roughly a hundred feet by fifty feet by a hundred feet. It was surrounded by busy streets and serviced by what seemed like fifty buses each hour. There was one small covered pavilion for bus passengers that Neal occasionally used as a shelter when it rained. A gray wooden rail fence decorated most of the perimeter, except where bus passengers and other pedestrians walked. Constant noise came from the passing cars and idling buses, though it wasn't an obnoxious roar.

Only longtime Cambridge residents ever knew Neal's Island by its official name, William Dawes Park. On the island, decorative monuments explained the history of the city of Cambridge from the days of George Washington.

One half of the island was surfaced with smooth red-and-black bricks, while grass and little plants grew in between the old, light-gray stones paving the other half. Several brass horseshoes were embedded in the concrete sidewalk that cut through the middle of the island.

Neal preferred to relax on his island rather than in the spot in front of CVS because, despite the traffic, it was more peaceful, had longer benches he could lie on, and had hundreds of daylilies and iris plants where he stashed personal items, such as milk jugs filled with water to rinse off with, a couple of potted plants he carefully looked after, and a blanket. "Don't knock down the flowers," he had warned me when he showed me how to secretly stash my own things in the daylilies.

He treated the island and Harvard Square like his own home. In effect, it was. When he once showed me pictures he had developed from a disposable camera — as one might show off a family photo album — the pictures were of his homeless friends and flowers around Harvard Square.

Neal was particularly protective of a wild sunflower that grew along the fence in back of the daylilies on Neal's Island. I'm not sure if he planted the seed there or not, but he looked after it with the enthusiasm of a parent. With his own spade, he had dug up and replanted flower bulbs where he thought they would look prettier. He told me later that the city replaced the bulbs on the island regularly and always left some behind accidently. Neal's health was poor and he thought he'd be dead by the next summer, so he told me that next year I could look at the flowers that he'd planted and remember him. Maybe Neal was afraid of someday being forgotten.

Neal was usually the center of attention on his island, at least among his friends. Thousands of others who walked or drove by may have thought of him as just a bum. Sometimes Neal would rest on the ground in the mulch on his island under the scarce shade of a sickly crabapple tree, but he was never bothered by the cars passing by less than six feet away. But then, Neal rarely seemed bothered by anything, except loneliness and occasional problems with others on the streets.

After Neal and I walked from CVS to Neal's Island, Neal talked to Ricky, who had been stemming in traffic and was resting on a bench. I saw Neal give Ricky four one-dollar bills; then Ricky gave Neal a little wooden cross, about three inches long on a thin, glittery rope. I don't know how they negotiated the price or what inspired Ricky even to have a cross for Neal to buy. But four dollars seemed like a lot for that little cross. I also thought about how Ricky would just use Neal's money to buy heroin. But maybe I was wrong.

Then Neal looked at me and said, "Here, I want to give this to you, John." He reached his hand out toward me, still clutching the cross. Neal looked up toward heaven and prayed, "God, please protect John as he's out here on the streets this summer." The sincerity of his voice and his prayer clashed with the surroundings of Neal's Island. I don't recall exactly what he said now, but I remember that he blessed it in the name of Jesus of Nazareth and then presented it to me. And although I didn't want to take it at first, I'm glad I did. It has since become one of my most precious keepsakes.

While the cross is a symbol of hope, it's also a symbol of brokenness — the brokenness of us all. Just as Jesus' body was broken for our sins, the cross reminds us that we, too, are broken. It symbolizes our wrongs, our selfishness, and our impurities, in contrast to Jesus' righteousness, selflessness, and holiness. The cross reminds us that whoever we are — rich or poor, living in a mansion or on the streets — we're in need of a savior. It is at the foot of the cross that we place our shame and regret and failure, and ask God to resurrect them into something new. That in and of itself may be difficult, because putting down our failures is sometimes not easy. Other times, the distractions and temptations of life blind us so that we don't see the reality of our brokenness. Sometimes that brokenness is clouded by an inflated sense of our own morality. The cross is where repentance and resurrection meet, where we learn about, or recalibrate ourselves to, the Jesus way. It's where we're reminded that on our own, we may live unhappily, but with Jesus, we can be free to live abundantly. It is in that awareness and subsequent transformation that we can find fresh hope, realizing that the words of Jesus "are full of the Spirit and life" (John 6:63).

Maybe Neal bought the cross to remind me about what he'd said moments before: "You need to praise God every day you have life." Or maybe he gave it to me so that I'd have something by which to remember God, as well as himself. I kept that wooden cross in my pocket every day that summer and it was always there to remind me that Neal was my friend. Over the weeks, the glittery rope got so badly tangled up in my pocket with the string of another cross that to this day, it's still a knotted mess.

In the words of

NEAL

I've got two things in my life: Jesus and music. The beer is just a sidekick. My most prized possession is my '62 Harmony guitar. I just got it a few months ago. It doesn't look like much, but it just has a nice sound to it. I like it. And it reminds me of my childhood. My mother told me my whole life that I should've been an actor. I love film. I'd love to be an actor. But because of my health, I always feel like, What's the point of doing stuff? I've got to get over that. That's my biggest problem — feeling like, What's the use of doing anything because I'm going to die anyway? You know what I mean, that feeling?

I love so many movies, but *Forrest Gump* is the greatest movie ever made. It's like an epic film. He does everything in life. And then Jenny. She died of AIDS. And she asked *him* to marry *her*. After all those years, never another woman — only Jenny. And he runs across the country for three years, and then all of a sudden he stops — in the middle of the desert — and he goes, "Think I'll go home now."

And there's a movie with Joe Pesci. It's a good movie. He lives in the boiler room underneath one of the Harvard buildings. Some guy asks who he is, and Joe Pesci goes, "I'm a bum. But ... I'm a Harvard bum."

I love Harvard Square; it's very artistic. I meet people from all over the world, but I don't like the junkies and jerks that hang around there. I don't want to be around negative people.

Rumors go around Harvard Square. You don't know what to believe from all these street people. I come back from LA every year — I don't stay here in the winter — and they go, "Neal, hey, man, good to see you. I heard you were dead. I heard you died in the VA hospital."

"No, I'm alive."

People just talk about you behind your back. People have said bad things about me because they're jealous. That's a sin. They go, "What's so special about Neal? Everyone loves Neal." And they make up stories about you — you did something, or whatever. And people come to me and go, "Did you do that?"

When I was sick, some guys wanted to beat me up. One of my friends goes, "You ever touch this man, I'll kill you," to these guys. He was protecting me when I was sick. I couldn't even move. They just wanted to start a fight because they were drunks. It's awful. I don't bother anybody.

Most of the homeless street people have mental issues, low self-esteem, all these different issues. Jesus took that all away from me. One time, I was really down and out. I prayed, "Jesus, if you're really listening, take these negative thoughts. Jesus, I'm yours now. I can't live without you. I'm tired of being depressed all the time. I give up." And he took it away. When you're down and out, your prayer gets heard. Jesus came for the downtrodden.

Drinking has gotten in the way of my life. But in a way, drinking has made me more comfortable. I know people are concerned about me, but it goes in one ear and out the other about drinking the beer. I don't drink those big forties anymore. I drink no malt liquor. I drink regular beer now. It has much less alcohol.

My life is an open book, and I take one minute at a time. Sometimes I don't know what to do, and I ask God and the answer comes. I just feel it. The only way I know how to ever be a success is through my Christ. I know that's the truth, because that's all I have left.

I feel it's important to spread the word of Jesus of Nazareth. I wish everyone was a Christian because I believe that the Christian church is the first church and the only church. Even though I drink too much beer — I'm a drink-too-much-beer Christian, that's all I can say — I keep my faith. I gave myself to him a long time ago. I basically said, "You know what? I'm nothing without you. Here I am; take me." Yeah, he still lets me suffer sometimes. You know why? Because of all my past stuff that I've done. But this is Satan's world. If Jesus was from this world, he would fix everything. It's a big test. He gives us a beautiful plan and sees what we do with it.

Following Jesus is the hardest thing on the planet.

The cross means everything to me. I have a cross in my bag now; it's real small. I saw a picture of a cross in some local magazine, and Jesus was totally covered in blood. That's the way it was. He was tortured. He was almost dead even before they nailed him to the cross. And the whips they had — I read stuff about it by theologians — they had leather straps with little nails sticking out, and they whipped him — front and back and legs, everything.

I know he suffered for me. I'll never forget that.

In the words of

DANE

*I*f you are homeless, and you're in need and at the behest of the good graces of strangers, then you must portray yourself as such. When I was jocular with people, when I was panhandling, they'd say, "Well, you seem pretty happy for a homeless, hungry, broke guy."

And I'd go, "What, should I wallow in my misery and just be self-indulgent? Or should I get over myself and rise to the task? I'm a survivor. I'm an urban pioneer. I persevere. I don't just fall. I get back up. Isn't that enough for you? What shall I say to you that would elicit a much-needed dollar from you?"

And because I can't just sit there and do nothing like some people with a sign, hiding behind it, I have to entertain myself. Even if I'm broke and hungry and I'm trying to get food, I've got to enjoy asking for money. So that's where the routine comes from.

People would go by trying to text so they didn't have to look at me. And I'm like, "Text me a sandwich, hun? What is it, No Quarters for the Bum Tuesday? Cause I didn't get the memo, you guys. My fax is down. Yeah, my whole house is down. I'm homeless!" I would just warble. And people would stop, and they'd listen to me for a few minutes and say, "Love your spiel," and give me five bucks and say, "You're very clever."

In Harvard Square, there were tourists from all over the world — the haves. And I soon realized when I used to panhandle down by the Harvard Square subway stop that a lot of students would give me their gold dollar coins that they'd get from the machine downstairs. They'd put money in the machine to enrich their card and they'd get coins. In a way, it seemed that that was their way of like cleansing their soul — *just give the bum the goldies* — their way of feeling like they're giving something back. The thing with the goldies is that they're like a burden. You wish that the machine would give dollar bills back. Now you've got all this weight in your pocket. And what better way to serve two purposes — first your own — you get it out of your pocket; you're not just going to throw it away. You can purge yourself of it in a way that you can feel like you are doing something to contribute to a problem that you see. And that's a good thing, and I always appreciated it. But I just had a sense that people give for different reasons. And you can see the reason as they're giving, whether it's pure, whether it's adulterated, whether it's just off the cuff, or whatever. You can see what it is that's moving people towards you. And so you learn. I'm a chameleon. I'll become whatever it is or whatever it takes to get the thing done. I have all those abilities, but also the ability to read what's going on.

I remember one time standing in Harvard Square, and this woman in her fifties or so was walking by, and she had this gorgeous, silver-gray-platinum hair. And I said to her, "Boy, you make gray look great! And she didn't acknowledge me for three more steps. Then she stopped and she turned, and she looked directly at me, and she said, "Were you speaking to me, sir?"

And I said, "None other than you."

She just lit up like a Christmas tree. She turned and walked off, and she looked different. And I said to myself, she's going to take that glow home, and she's going to tell somebody there that this man just said the most wonderful thing to me. And I thought about that and I said, yeah, that's what I do. That's what Dane does. I try to show people themselves through someone else's eyes, that they might see themselves through my eyes. I try to show people their strength, and point out the positive aspects of their lives.

When you're homeless, there's only one place that you can be absolutely alone — a public bathroom. Even then, there's always somebody knocking on the door trying to get in. I would go to the Red Doors Church's bathroom and use the facilities and clean up as best I could, take a cat bath in the sink with soap and a washcloth. Every now and then, if it was really hot and I was really dirty, there's a drain in the floor of the bathroom in the church, and I used to strip down and scrub my whole body, with a washcloth and soap, and then pour buckets of water over my head and let it run down the drain. I'd be in that room for thirty-five minutes, and I would take a shower in there. Then once I got clean, it was time to find something to eat. I'd get to that panhandle spot, raise enough money to get food and a little pot. And then I would be good. I didn't drink. I didn't smoke cigarettes.

I'm more accepted by young people than people my own age. One of the young kids who used to hang out in Harvard Square used to call me "the coolest old dude in the galaxy." People my own age don't get me. I'm like some throwback to the sixties. But so what? What should I be?

At one point in my life, everything was private and secret,

because it was all despicable, and I didn't want people to know the things I had to do to get cocaine. I was ashamed of myself. Now my life is open. Before I was closed and cloistered, and I only took; I didn't give. And now that I have been freed from that obsession to chase cocaine, I am allowed through this God-given freedom to live as people live every day.

I have no limitations in what I talk about in my life. My life is an open book at this juncture. There is nothing to hide or protect or defend. I have no compunction about revealing despicable activities. It's all part of my growth and development. I was there; I did that. And although I do feel a bit of shame when I acknowledge it, I also feel the purification of letting it be cleansed in the light of day. I am a different man today. If someone can learn from what I have endured, so that they need not go through the same thing, then herein lies my very self.

Three

FREEDOM AND FRIENDS

A loud boom reverberated throughout the park. I seemed to be the only one still trying to sleep in Cambridge Common, a grassy park filled with monuments and plaques commemorating the past, and used for sports, picnicking, and, for some homeless people, sleeping. It was the Fourth of July, and later that day George told me in a proud kind of way, "You're right where it all began, John." We were in the same place that George Washington and countless other patriots had fought for freedom in the war before America's birthday.

About fifty yards from where I woke that morning is a display honoring General George Washington, near where he gathered the colonies' soldiers in July 1775. He inspected them under a large elm tree, gave a speech pronouncing them the new Continental Army, and called them to engage in the common cause of freedom. A younger elm tree grows there now, and an old granite monument states, "Under This Tree Washington First Took Command of the American Army, July 3, 1775."

Three large cannons, abandoned by the British soldiers when they evacuated Boston in 1776, stand prominently nearby. Signs on Neal's Island state how during the night of April 18, 1775 — the night Paul Revere warned of the British attack — a patriot named William Dawes (the man for whom Neal's Island is technically named) galloped by on his way to Lexington to also warn of the attack. The brass horseshoes embedded in the sidewalk on Neal's Island commemorate his ride. The signs state that not long after Dawes's memorable ride, thousands of men moved to Cambridge, living all around the city, including in some of Harvard's buildings and in barracks built on the Cambridge Common. In June of that year, soldiers gathered on the Common before leaving to fight the British in the Battle of Bunker Hill. The mission for freedom was in high gear.

George was right. We *were* where it all began.

Living in Boston and Cambridge, you can't help but feel the sense of history all around. I remember walking with Chubby John and one of our other friends around Boston one spring evening. Chubby John led us along some of the Freedom Trail, through Boston's North End, telling stories of growing up in the area. As we neared Paul Revere's home, Chubby John recited a Longfellow poem he had learned in elementary school: "Listen my children and you shall hear of the midnight ride of Paul Revere.... One if by land, and two if by sea; and I on the opposite shore will be."

A number of people from Harvard Square gathered for a Fourth of July party at someone's house, and George invited me to come along. When Neal wanted to leave to go to the party, I helped him put his cart on the bus; it was too heavy for one person to lift, and almost too heavy for two people, but we got it on the bus, and he somehow maneuvered it off the bus okay, though later he told me he forgot to pay the bus fare.

George gave me directions to the party, and walking there later, I picked up old scratch-off lottery tickets from the sidewalk. Picking up discarded tickets provided an element of excitement. *Would I find a winning ticket?* Neal had told a story of his friend who had success pulling winners out of trash cans, and I heard that Jared had struck twenty dollars recently simply by looking at a discarded scratch-off ticket someone had misread as a loser. One time, Chubby John scolded me as we walked from his campsite to the subway because I had lingered looking for tickets.

"Quit picking up all those tickets, John. It'll drive you nuts looking at them all the time!" He did have a point, and I never found a winning ticket.

After finding the house where the party was, several of us sat on black milk crates in a circle in the back yard. Chicken wings and BBQ ribs cooked on the grill while Neal lay on a slab of cement singing a Pink Floyd song with his eyes closed and repeating his new joke about what hell would be like: trapped in a prison cell for eternity, plagued by the words of Becky, a young woman who stemmed next to CVS, "Spare change, spare change, spare change." He repeated the words in a nasal voice just like hers, drawing out each word.

A radio, lodged in an upstairs window, blared music into the back yard. A number of young people who hung out in the Harvard Square "pit," a brick-laid terrace next to the main entrance of the

Harvard Square subway station, attended the party too. For decades that area by the subway had been called "the pit," I suppose because some of the area was lower than street level. The pit provided an optimum place in Harvard Square for smoking, talking, and playing hacky sack. But it wasn't just a place; it defined a culture.

Some who hung out in the pit were minors; others were in their twenties. Some were homeless, or semi-homeless, while others were travelers. They often called themselves pit rats and came from various walks of life that led them to an alternative lifestyle that included hanging out with other like-minded individuals and sometimes using drugs. Some would sit on the sidewalks and stem for money, holding signs with clever statements such as "I bet you $1 you'll read this." Sometimes I'd meet adults who had spent time in the pit when they were young and still hung around Harvard Square.

Some of the people from the pit had trouble with their home life. Some decided to leave home on their own; others because they had to. Many just came to the pit when they wanted to. A few months before the summer began, Bernard gave me a microwavable container chock-full of spaghetti and meat sauce, so full it almost eased out the sides with the lid fastened down. Someone from the pit had given it to him. Bernard said this guy's father had come out to talk to his son, bringing along dinner for him. For some reason, the son gave the food to Bernard. Maybe he thought Bernard needed it more than he did. Or maybe it was his way of passively rejecting his father. I sometimes still feel sad for that dad, and for the son for whom the spaghetti was intended, and for whatever situation they had found themselves in.

At the party, many of the young people were smoking a marijuana bowl in a pot circle and watching *Beavis and Butt-Head* reruns in the living room. A couple of people asked me if I smoked. Perhaps they would have shared with me, too, if I had said yes. Everyone at the party was free to do as they wished. They smoked what they wanted, drank what they wanted, and talked how they wanted.

I didn't know many of the people at the party, but one person I was glad to see was Bob, who ultimately ended up attending my Harvard graduation. Bob was an older gentleman who always carried around a sack or two full of national newspapers such as the *Wall Street Journal*. His hair was always uncombed and his face was covered with a long beard. The only other time I had met him was around midnight one night when I was sitting in the pit writing in my journal. He came off the subway and I nodded to him from a distance. From several yards away, he held up a small package of shrimp shumai as if to ask, "Could I offer you something?"

"It's got shrimp in it. Somebody gave it to me," he said, suggesting that he didn't need it or that I might not like it. But I gladly accepted the snack.

I always felt comfortable around Bob because he was so calm and friendly. Bob didn't seem to have any addictions or problems, and he never gave anyone any trouble. He spent most of each day away from Harvard Square, reading his newspapers. I never knew where he slept, and never asked him.

At the party, Teresa remembered that I had let her borrow my sleeping bag a couple of nights before and thanked me.

"Teresa has a nice face," Neal told me later, "but she's too ..." His voice dropped and he stretched his arms out. "I saw pictures of her when she was younger, and she was beautiful," he said.

I laid down on the cement slab to relax — as best as I could on the hard surface — next to where Neal had been resting. I took out flash cards with words such as *algunas*, *hermano*, and *pero*, which

I had made to study for my Spanish class. Passing my language requirement was, in theory, my first priority that summer, since that was the only thing standing between me and my degree. I was never good at language courses, despite following the advice of a former professor, who had suggested to his students that we redeem our spare time by studying vocabulary flash cards. At Harvard, I struggled with passing the language component required in my program. Had I passed, I would have already graduated and wouldn't have been taking this Spanish class, or been in Cambridge, for that matter. I needed to do well — no, I *had* to do well — in order to graduate. My master's program was supposed to be completed in one year, and this class felt like my last attempt at survival. Yet friends and the distractions of the streets were more interesting than studying Spanish. Blending the two, when possible, seemed the perfect solution.

I relaxed with my flash cards in hand. "Have you ever been married?" I asked Neal.

"For one year," he replied, sitting on the concrete in front of me. "We were still friends after we divorced," he was quick to add, noting they hadn't talked in a long time. It was as if Neal was unhappy about it all. He hated divorce. "Divorce is an abomination to the Lord," he once told me. But at the time of his divorce, he was using cocaine. My guess was that his spirit was befuddled since his marriage had ended, whatever the circumstances had been.

"I couldn't handle marriage," Neal later told me. "I was irresponsible. I told my wife, 'You know what? I can't be married anymore,' basically. She cried. I paid some lawyer six hundred bucks to divorce her. I felt so bad. I cried. I felt like a stupid jerk. It just didn't work out."

Neal always seemed like he wanted someone in his life to love. But when we talked about it, you'd think he wasn't sure. One time I asked him, "Do you ever want to have a woman to love?"

"I already do," he said. "I love all my women friends." Then he paused. "Do you mean romantically?"

"Yeah," I said.

"That's not my intention. I don't want to be tied down with one woman."

His answer surprised me, but in some ways it also made sense. Neal was a man on the move. He'd move across the country when the weather got cold or spend a few days at his mother's home when he wanted to or felt he needed time off the streets. But after a little while, he always returned to Harvard Square.

After I left the Fourth of July party, I met some non-homeless friends to watch the fireworks, and hung out with my friend Josh at a restaurant until late into the night. Along with spending time with my homeless friends that summer, I continued to maintain close connections with my non-homeless friends. And my summer language course landed me in class three nights a week. That summer, I didn't extricate myself from my normal life as a student, which included a lot of time on the internet and in the library. My homeless friends sometimes used the internet, as well, and spent time with friends or relatives, and watched television or took showers at friends' homes, when given the opportunity.

It's not accurate for me to say I was homeless, even though I didn't have any dorm or apartment to stay in that summer. I spent time on the streets voluntarily, and those who were truly homeless usually had no other choice. I was a student with no conditions or addictions pinning me to the streets. And whereas my experience ended before summer turned to fall, some who were really homeless knew they'd still be out there perhaps much longer. I shall forever be thankful to the homeless people who befriended me that summer, those who spent time with me, those who journeyed with me as we explored life together, those whom I was able to learn with, from, and about. Neal was one of those people.

The day after the Fourth of July party, I found Neal sitting along the side of the wide sidewalk beside the black iron fence of the cemetery in Harvard Square. He was sitting peacefully, his cart next to him on his right, and a cup sitting in front of him.

The sun was finally bright, the temperature warm, and the Square bustled with Sunday shoppers and Independence Day sightseers. Recently, though, chatter on the streets had been all about the cold weather we'd been having.

"I can't believe how cold it is," Neal had said. "This gloomy stuff makes me get the blues." We'd look up at the sky and somebody would say wishfully, "I think the sun is getting ready to come out. I see a patch of blue." Then Neal would sing "Stormy Weather" and the chorus of "Tomorrow," from the musical *Annie*. Bernard had said, "It's almost July and gotta wear a sweater, and in two months it'll be time to wear a sweater again." Neal had bought a full-length black North Face winter coat for twenty dollars from somebody. "It's pretty bad I gotta wear this North Face coat and still be chilly," he'd said as he listened to the Beatles on his headphones. He'd talk about moving to Los Angeles and dream about going to Brazil because he had had enough of the weather. "Brazilian women are gorgeous," he'd add several times.

Neal was Neal—always feeling free to do as he pleased and say what he wished. People liked Neal, and he made me laugh a lot that summer. One morning, three charter buses full of high school students from Illinois pulled up in front of CVS. Neal greeted several of them as they came off the bus: "Welcome to Harvard; I'm your tour guide!"

And I remember what Simon, the leader among the young people from the Harvard Square pit, had said about Neal the first time I met him. He and I had a short conversation late at night, when the busyness of the Square had died down, employees and shoppers had long gone home, the silence from the lack of street performers and students created a sense of loneliness, and some of the only sounds you heard were buses, the chirping walk signal, and idling engines from a few taxis awaiting customers. "You know who's my friend?" Simon asked. "Neal's my friend. Cause he's consistent."

Neal and I sat on the sidewalk next to the cemetery's fence for most of that Sunday afternoon. When I saw him, he had been sitting there for two hours and had only one dollar in his cup. Pretty soon, a man with a dog walked by and put a five-dollar bill in it. Maybe Neal had met him before; I don't remember. Or perhaps it was the nice weather, or maybe we had greeted him or asked him if he had any spare change, or maybe he just felt like extending some charity. If someone walked by and put money in the cup, we'd thank them heartily.

For Neal, stemming always seemed secondary to enjoying the afternoon in the shade of the cemetery's Norway maple tree that extended its branches over the brick sidewalk. On that Sunday afternoon, people gave $11.12 to Neal and me as we sat on the sidewalk. Yet enjoying time with friends always seemed more important to him than making money. Like some others, Neal received a benefits check each month from the government. Stemming for Neal usually consisted of relaxing with a cup in front of him. He told me, "Wherever I sit or sleep, I always put a cup out, because you never know. Somebody might put something in. One time, I went to sleep right in front of CVS. I woke up and there was fifteen dollars in it."

Money that people put in his cup was added value to his time spent relaxing or talking with friends.

We watched people walk by all afternoon, people of all ages and backgrounds. Neal told me, based on his experience, who was the least likely to give a handout and whom he doesn't even bother asking, because people from those groups had never given him anything. Yes, it was a lesson in generalities. He also said he doesn't ask for money from people with children, or the elderly.

At times, Neal used his humor to get the attention of a passerby. He'd say things like, "Spare a home for the changeless?" Neal did goofy things too, like squeeze a baby toy so that it squeaked and made people smile as they walked by. Sometimes he'd just set a doll or his Godzilla toy beside him to draw attention. Neal always wanted to make people laugh, and he'd laugh along with them. I think laughter may have been like a medicine for the things that sometimes got him down.

Neal loved telling jokes too. Once, when we were standing along Massachusetts Avenue in front of CVS, just down from the Harvard Coop bookstore, he asked me, "Why did the chicken cross Mass. Ave.?... To get to the Coop." And then he'd laugh out loud, sometimes tilting his head back, widening his eyes, or using his hands expressively to point at me. He liked that joke so well he might have told it to me three or four times that summer.

One time, he told several of us about how the night before, while he was sleeping in Cambridge Common, he got up and was walking in the park when he came across the body of a dead woman. He told the story dramatically, as if he were reliving the moment, and we listened intently, because Neal was telling us what I thought was news we hadn't yet heard. "Yeah, and there were seagulls eating her body," he said. *Seagulls?* I thought. *How could there be seagulls in*

Cambridge Common in the middle of the night? "Then the police came," Neal said, "and they started to eat the woman too."

Neal told me that he liked "road dog friends," people who would stick around and talk, not just come around for an hour and leave. A couple of times, after visiting with him for a short time, I told him I was heading to the library or somewhere else for a while. "Oh, good, I can be alone all day," he'd say, as if I had betrayed our friendship. Perhaps his friends and jokes and dreams of better living covered any hurt he had from past experiences or relationships, like his short marriage.

Among the thousands of people who walked by that particular Sunday afternoon was a young woman, Amy, who had just graduated with a master's degree from Harvard. I had commented about a travel book she was carrying, and soon she sat down on the sidewalk with us and talked about how she was going to be traveling to Europe with some friends for her summer vacation. She had a small loaf of carrot bread wrapped in aluminum foil that she had made for a friend. For some reason — maybe the friend wasn't home or maybe she changed her mind or maybe she just liked Neal and me — she gave the bread to us instead. And with our conversation that day, and the extension of homemade hospitality, Amy became one of our "road dog friends" that summer. She came back the next day, saying she missed us and was afraid she'd never see us again. She even stemmed with Neal that next day and they made seven dollars together. She repeated her visits to see us, occasionally sharing pieces of coffee cake and slices of banana bread. She always brought a jolly smile to the streets that made her glow like a little girl meeting Santa Claus.

The same Sunday we met Amy, a woman walked up to us carrying a backpack and a couple of bottles stashed inside a plastic bag. She wanted to talk. She *needed* to talk. She told us that she had recently spent time in the hospital after being hurt in an accident, that she was an alcoholic, and that she had been rejected by both of her daughters. Doris was a skinny woman, around sixty-five years old, and had short, curly gray hair on which a little blue-rimmed bonnet was perfectly placed. She looked like she had jumped out of the picture on a box of Little Debbie snack cakes and aged fifty years.

I had just seen Doris in the Cambridge Common at the Outdoor Church, a service that meets each Sunday at 1:00 p.m. and caters to homeless people. People gather there together to pray, talk, and share in the Lord's Supper — a wafer and juice distributed in little cups. After the brief service, everyone enjoys sandwiches, prepared by people from local churches, and juice boxes. Then the pastors spend the rest of the afternoon giving out sandwiches and clothes to people on the streets of Cambridge, sharing words of encouragement. I hold a lot of respect for the tireless efforts of the pastors and interns who serve the homeless, week after week, in all seasons and temperatures.

During the questions and discussion time of the service, Doris asked in a southern accent, "What if I believe in God and I'm wrong?"

"What do you have to lose?" Dane answered. Dane knew the value of faith in God. He believed that God had been able to do things in his life that he'd not been able to do on his own, such as deliver him from the throes of a cocaine addiction. He had an ability to reflect on his life and regrets in a way that I'd come to connect with when reflecting on my own.

Only in her second day in Harvard Square, Doris seemed comfortable being herself with all of us strangers. She asked the ministers if we could sing "Amazing Grace," which was printed at the end of the order of worship page that they had handed out to us, each in a plastic sleeve. After we finished singing it, she said, "Thank you for letting me smile today. I didn't think I would."

After the service, I watched someone give Doris a few coins. She didn't feel comfortable accepting the money, though, as if she didn't feel she needed it, or as if she felt she wasn't in a worse position than the man extending the charity.

"Accept it as a gift from God," Dane reasoned with her. "He wants to help you. You're homeless."

Doris was humbled. "I don't know where I'll sleep tonight," she said, perhaps as a way to justify accepting the money.

A couple of hours later, when Doris asked if she could join Neal and me on the sidewalk, Neal was lying down, sleeping, but soon woke up to meet our new visitor.

"Are you homeless?" Neal asked her.

"I'm definitely homeless," Doris said. "I slept in the Coop last night."

"Well, you're sleeping with us tonight," he said, as a way to welcome her to Harvard Square.

Doris then recounted how it had felt to sit hopelessly on the sidewalk the day before, holding a sign and a paper cup. "Isn't it amazing how you can become invisible?" Doris asked, noting how homeless people sitting on the sidewalk are often ignored. "It takes multiple humiliations to get one dollar sitting here on the streets. But if you're well-dressed and you need to get on the subway — but you forgot your wallet at home — you would get it."

I had also been thinking earlier that day about people who had walked by without looking at us. I don't think they were trying to be rude; they may have just not known how to react to us. I understood how seeing a homeless person sitting on the street might be uncomfortable. And in our society today, people don't typically greet or even look at everyone they pass on the streets; they mind their own business. People passing by us might think, *Why should I look at people sitting on the sidewalk if I don't even look at the people who are* walking *on the sidewalk?* And since people often question what will be done with money they give to strangers, someone might ask, *Will the money be used for the wrong purpose? Will my act of goodwill ultimately hurt the one I'm trying to help?*

After a little while, the three of us started singing, "It's a beautiful day in the neighborhood," and Beatles songs — Neal's favorite — as if none of us had a care in the world. But I knew that wasn't the case. Doris poured the remainder of a large bottle of vodka into a thirty-two-ounce Big Gulp cup from 7-Eleven and poured in some soda to mix with it.

"Oh, you drink vodka?" I asked.

"Yeah, I hate it," she said.

I think I was realizing more the power of addiction, yet it was hard to understand why she was harming herself that way. Alcohol was a way for many on the streets to bury their problems, to make everything seem better. But it always made things worse.

Doris needed friends, and she needed to talk. She knew that I studied theology, and she had studied it some in college too, somewhere in Texas. "What are your favorite Bible passages?" she asked me.

I thought about it for a minute. It wasn't every day that someone asked me about my favorite parts of the Bible. "I really like the story of Elijah and the prophets of Baal in the Old Testament," I responded, telling the story to her. Then I asked her the same question, and after she responded, I talked about how I saw creation, along with my view of how sin entered and disturbed God's good order. "God had told people not to sin, but human beings did what they wanted to do," I said. "The penalty and result for doing sin was death. So God, in God's mercy and love, decided to come into the world to do for people what they could not do for themselves — die and solve the sin problem. And then Jesus rose from the dead as a way to show that nothing — not even death — could conquer him. Through Jesus, we can have our sins forgiven, and God's original desire that people live forever is restored, in heaven."

Then I told her a story I once heard on the radio. "Imagine you're driving a car and you're going too fast. A police officer pulls you over and writes you a big ticket for speeding. But you tell the officer, 'I'm poor. I have no way of paying this ticket.' The police officer thinks about it for a moment and starts having pity for you and says, 'Here, why don't you give me that ticket back. I'm going down to the courthouse right now and I'll pay it for you.' At first, you're confused. *Why would a police officer who just gave me a ticket want to pay it for me out of his own pocket?*

"That's how I like to see God," I told her. "As doing for me what I could not do for myself."

Doris seemed to enjoy our conversation and talking about theology. Before we departed later that day, she told me why she wanted to talk.

Although her mind was sharp, Doris commented about how easy it was to lose things on the streets, including her reading glasses. She told me that since the vodka had taken its effect on her, she was unable to walk down the street to CVS to purchase a new set herself. So she gave me money and told me the exact kind she needed. After I returned with her new glasses, we talked for a while before she asked another favor from me.

"I've got one more request for a run," she said.

"What's that?" I asked.

She wanted to give me money to buy her another bottle of vodka and soda. I told her I could show her the liquor store, but I wasn't going to buy vodka for her. If she really wanted it, she'd have to go in and buy it herself. Unfortunately, she did.

Maybe Neal's drinking exaggerated my reaction to Doris's drinking that first day I met her. The way I saw it, Doris was depending on something that was hurting her, though I hadn't had the same troubles that had led her to start drinking in the first place. All the while, I was starting to see dependence in a new light — dependence as something we're all guilty of, just in different ways and degrees. It seems everyone, in some way, is dependent on something. For some it's alcohol or cigarettes or drugs; for others it's friends or the internet or coffee — whatever. Neal said that some people are addicted to their cell phones.

I walked Doris down the street toward the liquor store. She held on to my arm as she staggered alongside me, as if her legs were heavy and ready to give out at any moment.

"I'm afraid of dying," she said. "That's why I wanted to talk to you today."

"So you're gonna go in there and buy something that's contributing to your death?" I asked her.

"No, I'm postponing my death," she said. "I have to have it. I'll get the shakes in the morning if I don't."

I had heard about the shakes. George had told me about how severe alcoholics, whose bodies are so used to alcohol, can go into seizures if they don't drink what their bodies demand.

We'd walked the short distance to the store. "There it is," I said, pointing to it.

"Are you going to be here when I get out?" she asked.

"I've got to go. I've got things to do," I said, in a way that probably conveyed my disappointment and disapproval. Right or wrong—and maybe it was more wrong than right—I left her in front of the store and walked away. For the remainder of the summer, Doris was in Harvard Square to stay. And so was her drinking.

It was my fourteenth day on the streets, and in that short walk with Doris, who was barely able to walk and talking about dying, a different kind of emotion flooded my mind—a combination of anger and distress. My spirit felt as worn as the tread on my old Asics. Seeing the addiction of alcohol personified in her, and knowing that it prowled through the streets like the angel of death, troubled me in a way I'm not sure I'd ever felt troubled before.

One day, later in the summer, Doris and I talked on the bench in front of CVS. "The last time I saw you, you had stopped drinking for like thirty-six hours," I told her, expressing my frustration. "Now look at you. You said you wanted to stop drinking. You said you were going to stop."

"It's not that easy to stop," she replied. "I'll get the shakes."

"You were off it for thirty-six hours," I reminded her again. "That was pretty good."

"The onus of responsibility is not on anyone else," she told me. "I'm responsible for my problem."

"You know, when I reflect on what is the most difficult thing out here for me," I said, "yeah, it's been cold and rainy, but what has bothered me the most is seeing people destroy themselves."

I felt concerned about those who I thought were hurting themselves. Neal's situation wasn't as obvious as Doris's because he didn't drink hard liquor, and he carried on with life as if he were happy.

I didn't know then how badly Neal's body was suffering from other serious health problems. Before the summer was over, though, I would find out.

four

DANGER IN THE DARK

To commemorate a now-famous speech Ralph Waldo Emerson gave to the graduating class of Harvard Divinity School in 1838, the school hosts an outdoor popsicle party each July. It's a low-key Harvard tradition. No cakes. No punch. Just popsicles handed out from large plastic coolers outside the doors of the divinity school library. The year 2009 marked the speech's 171st anniversary, and I invited Hank, one of our street companions, to join me.

Hank, when he was younger, had hung out in the pit. As an adult, he continued spending time in Harvard Square during the day. At night, though, he slept indoors, usually in his friend Graham's apartment, and sometimes at a relative's home.

Hank's experiences came alive with his expressive and passionate personality. His gestures complemented his excitement about whatever he talked about, and he often spoke frankly about how he saw the world. Hank's crass vocabulary and conversation were also peppered with his prolific use of the f-word. It was as much a part of his vocabulary as the word *the* was a part of anyone else's.

Hank once told me, "If you can count the number of true friends on more than one hand, you're a lucky dog."

One night, after I returned from my evening class, I found Hank, Neal, Chubby John, Doris, Teresa, and several others in front of CVS, singing and laughing. They told me of the big party they'd had, of the Bob Dylan, Beatles, and folk songs they'd sung, and of the food and fun I had just missed. A street singer from out of town had played his guitar, and Neal had played the tambourine.

When I arrived, Hank was cooking the last hamburger on Neal's George Foreman Grill. "You hungry?" he asked me. "I'll split my burger with you." Hank could have told me there weren't any extras, but he didn't. He shared his with me. I'll never forget that.

On our short walk to the divinity school, Hank and I talked about methadone and methamphetamine. Maybe we had seen Melanie, a pregnant woman who stemmed in Harvard Square. Melanie was usually half-asleep each time I saw her. One time, I had seen her fall asleep — and nearly fall over — while standing up holding an ice cream cone. Ice cream dripped onto the bench she leaned against as she dozed off. Hank told me this sort of thing happened when people were taking methadone as a treatment for their heroin addiction, using heroin itself, or taking a combination of prescription medicines that induced sedation, giving a heroin-like effect.

After we returned from getting popsicles, Melanie was asking for "pins."

"What's that?" I asked Hank, when the two of us were alone.

"Klonopins," Hank told me, naming some of the prescription "benzos," or benzodiazepines, some addicts use. Hank told me that the pills are taken together, forming what is called a cocktail that costs about eight dollars on the streets.

There was a lot I didn't know — and still don't know — about street drugs. And even though I felt like I knew a little more after talking with Hank on our walk, I really didn't know as much as I thought I knew.

After ten o'clock that night, several of us hung around in front of CVS, watching the taxis line up along the curb on Mass. Ave. Then a man appeared. My back was to him, but I heard him ask in a bold, staggering voice, "Anybody got a pen?"

I guess it's not an unusual question to ask people you don't know. If there were a list of the top ten questions you'd ask strangers when you needed something, it would surely be on there. But my first impression wasn't that the stranger was asking for a pen; it was that he was asking for a pin, a Klonopin.

I pegged him as someone who wanted to know if we had drugs for sale, since Harvard Square was known as a place to buy them. I had assumed, because of the late hour and his tone, that he was some kind of substance abuser. He stood there for a few seconds, awaiting an answer. Then I thought, *Maybe he is asking for a pen.* I turned around halfway and said from the bench, "Oh, you mean something to write with?" I took the Bic pen from my pocket and showed it to him. "Here you go," I said and handed it to him. "But I need it back," I added. "It's the only one I have."

I'll admit, I've always been a bit obsessed about keeping my possessions safe and feel it's important to return what I borrow from others. It seems reasonable. If I borrow something from someone, I return it. If someone borrows something from me, that person returns it. But I learned at an early age that's not always the way it works.

When I was in middle school, clipped into my school binder was a zippered green-fabric pencil case full of pencils and pens. I must have been among the few in the school who had such a collection, because other students asked me almost every day, "Hey, John, can I borrow a pencil?" I knew that my friends might forget to return what they'd borrowed, so I implemented a collateral policy. It was simple. You borrow something from me, you give me something to borrow in return. When you return the pencil, I'll return your item. I probably learned it from one of my teachers, who had the same policy. Students would give him all kinds of things as collateral — even one of their shoes. I especially liked it when people gave me money as collateral, because sometimes a borrow turned into a sale. I had my own makeshift store in that little pencil case.

After I handed my pen to the stranger, instead of standing there using it and then promptly returning it, he walked away.

"Where you going with my pen?" I asked, my natural instincts and assumptions erupting in an accusing tone.

He turned around, but didn't say a word. Walking back toward me, he glared and tossed the pen at me. "I'll get my own," he said begrudgingly.

Now he didn't hurl the pen at me, but he certainly showed his displeasure at what I had thought was a perfectly reasonable question. When he walked away, though, I realized he was heading in the direction of the ATM at the bank next to CVS and probably would have returned the pen after conducting his business.

After a few minutes, he returned and sat down on the bench next to Neal and began talking with him as if they were old friends, although Neal was certain that he had never met the man before. Neal told me once that sometimes people will act friendly with him, like they've been buddies since they were kids, when all they want is a swig from his beer bottle. Maybe that was the case with this man.

The man leaned over and looked at me from the other side of Neal. "Here, I know you like pens," he said cynically. Then he tossed another pen at me. It hit my leg and bounced onto the brick sidewalk. I ignored it.

Hank walked over to me from behind, leaned down with his arm on the back of the bench, and said in a hushed voice, "I think that guy has it in for you. I'm keepin' my eye on him." I nonchalantly told Hank I wasn't worried.

"He said something to Chubby John about Neal's beer and about punching somebody over a pen," Hank added.

I had friends looking out for me, even though I didn't think the situation necessitated it. I hoped he would just leave. We all did.

A minute or two later, Hank called my name, in a sort of commanding way. Chubby John stood with him. "Hey, John, we're taking a walk. Come with us."

I didn't hesitate or ask any questions. I followed their directions, knowing they were pulling me from what they thought could be a dangerous situation. Chubby John said, "You never know what could happen. The best thing to do is just walk away."

They were right; you never knew what could happen on the streets. Before long, we'd see someone's beaten-up face and drops of blood spattered on the sidewalk that told the tale of something gone terribly wrong in our community.

I never saw the stranger again after that night. I didn't know anything about his story, where he was from, what problems he might have had, or what caused him to act the way he did.

That summer, I'm sure I didn't realize all of the potential there was for danger. Before the summer began, the one thing I feared was what could happen to me while I was sleeping, like getting kicked in the head when I was in my most vulnerable state. Harvard Square isn't the most dangerous place, though, and once the summer began, those fears mostly went away. Bad things did happen out on the streets, probably more often than I was aware. Certainly more could have happened. I suppose experiences from my past led me to understand the world that way.

It was Halloween night, and I was twelve years old. Dressed like a police officer, with a large badge, shiny handcuffs, and a brown holster holding a small silver gun that shot red paper caps, I bolted out of my house with a friend for some trick-or-treat fun.

But as we walked near our school, I saw out of the corner of my eye two boys running up to us from behind, their fists swinging and their mouths cursing. My attacker's face was puckered, and he looked as though he were possessed by the devil. He hit me twice, once in the jaw and then in the eye, and I fell on the blacktop road, clutching the pillowcase I was carrying to collect candy. It all happened so fast I hardly knew what happened, like slipping on ice and, in a split second, having your head and your toes switch places. Just as fast as they sneaked up on us, they ran off into the dark, crisp night, leaving us lying on the street like garbage from a fast food restaurant.

I suppose I did grow up in a town with its fair share of violence. We'd hear about teenage boys robbed of winter coats emblazoned with the colors of their favorite NFL teams. Gang presence increased in my school, and teens wore fire engine red clothes and hats to identify themselves as members of the Bloods. Kids in the other school wore blue, the color of the Crips.

A detective from the sheriff's department was even assigned to our school district to try to bring order to the fights and crimes that students committed. Although I wasn't involved in the dangerous crowd, I knew I could be one of their victims, just like anybody else.

That Halloween night, we quickly picked ourselves up off the street and committed to each other to tell the authorities. I had a bloody scrape on my right elbow and could feel pain on the left side of my face from a black eye that stayed for weeks. Although I wore sunglasses whenever possible, it was hard to hide the reality of an assault and battery when a shiner followed me around like a haunting shadow. I didn't go to school the next day. Soon, though, everyone knew what had happened.

Every day I'd walk to and from school past the place where the assault occurred. I was constantly frightened and worried that I might see my attacker on my paper route. What really gave me butterflies, though, was going to court hearings with my dad to see how the magistrate would dole out justice. Even though I never had to testify in person, it was nerve-racking to think about seeing my attacker there and being reminded of what had happened.

I never really knew the boy who hit me, and honestly, I never sought to understand his story. I only knew his name, his face, and his reputation. He was a year older than I was, and although we were about the same height, he was built like a lightweight boxer. I think he lived with his grandmother, and even at his young age, he was already notorious to school and law enforcement officials. He continued to involve himself in crime and wound up getting locked up for a long time in "juvie," as they called it, even escaping from there more than once. One time, he and some other detainees knocked over a guard, busted out of the door, and ran like chickens being chased by a butcher. They eluded the police for days, and articles in the newspaper warned readers and asked for tips to locate them. A couple of years after I graduated from high school, I heard on the radio that he — now a grown man — had died in a public park during a standoff with the city police. He shot at officers and they fired back at him fifteen times, but they found that he was killed by a self-inflicted gunshot wound to his head. The newspaper reported that he had had forty contacts with the police in a period of less than seven years for a range of crimes and was on the verge of a federal indictment for gang involvement.

Despite the anger I naturally had felt after the assault, I now think that he probably hadn't chosen a bad life himself; a bad life had chosen him, and the grip that it had on him ultimately pulled him to his death.

Many years have gone by since then, and I don't really know all the ways that experience shaped my life. Stories like mine remind me that certain events in our lives shape who we are. We may not talk about them. We may not even think about them all that often. But stories from our pasts have the power to churn our stomachs from shame and fear, or to electrify our hearts with cheer. Each of our lives is shaped by little stories that make up the bigger story of who we are. We're a composite of everything in our lives — both terrible and terrific, and everything in between — like a mosaic made up of tiny colored stones, each one representing a story or experience in a person's life. When it's all said and done, they make a picture, and that picture is you or me or a homeless person.

What someone's final mosaic will look like has yet to be determined. We don't think of mosaics as easily coming apart, but God's redemptive grace has the ability to transform our lives' mosaics into new pictures that look much different from the previous ones. We often feel that our mosaics — our stories — stick with us like bad tattoos. We either hide them, or we accept that we have them and move on with our lives, if we can. For some people, their stories are so painful that it's virtually impossible for them to move beyond them. They're unable to envision or move into a new mosaic. I wonder how many people I met on the streets who felt that way.

One night at 4:30 a.m., I was sleeping soundly on the grass in the Common when I heard Simon quietly speaking to someone as if they were having a chat in the middle of a sunny afternoon. Hearing that someone had been hurt, but not knowing what was going on, I called out to Simon. "Simon, who was it?"

"Oh, hey, is that Dave?" Simon asked.

"It's John."

"John, can I sit down?"

Simon sat down on the ground next to me, stretching his arm out and placing his left hand on the grass on the other side of me, as if he were tucking me in. Simon smelled as though he had had a fair amount of alcohol that night. "Three guys with masks messed up a guy who sleeps in my tent and the guy who's married to the 'spare change woman,'" he told me.

"Chet?" I asked.

"They messed him up. I just saw his wife."

Chet and I didn't know each other very well, but I often saw him and his wife, Becky, stemming next to CVS. I'm pretty sure Chet never knew my name, or much about me, and he never really seemed to care. He did know I was a student, though, and one time congratulated me about being accepted by the homeless community. "I heard you got your wings," he said, kiddingly.

Chet almost never smiled and his frosty personality may have been the result of the years he'd spent in prison. People said he and Becky slept on the porch of a nearby church, as well as behind the brick wall in back of the cemetery, a place thought to be one of the dirtiest spots in all of Harvard Square. Although it was private, Neal had told me, "So many people poop and pee back there, I wouldn't be caught dead there."

Might the same guys come through the park and beat me up too? I worried. I didn't know that Chet had been attacked several hours before, or any other details.

"Did they hurt you?" I asked Simon.

"No," he replied. Then, like an afterthought, he said, "I wish I didn't drink so much. I love you, man." Then he kissed me on the forehead.

"Love you too, man," I said.

Simon seemed to think that somehow the assault on the guy in his tent was connected with Chet's assault.

"I'm gonna go find them," he assured me. Then he paused.

"Oh, I should probably turn the other cheek, huh?" he asked.

"Well, yeah, but how are you going to find them?" I wondered, trying to help him rethink his plans.

"I don't know," he conceded. "But they're three guys with masks, unless they're wearing makeup. The cops are looking for them."

"Just let the police take care of it," I suggested.

"You're right, the police care so much about homeless people," he said sarcastically.

That wasn't the only time I had heard a cynical remark about the police. One time, I saw Neal lying on the bench on Neal's Island, but his cart wasn't with him.

"John, guess what?" he said, resting quietly with a cigarette between his fingers. "All my stuff got stolen. You know Jersey? She was watching my stuff for a couple hours. I gave her a forty," he said, explaining how he traded a bottle of beer in exchange for watching his cart while he went to the movie theater to watch *My Sister's Keeper*. Neal watched *My Sister's Keeper* four times that summer and cried each time. He strongly recommended that I watch it too. "It will change your life," he had assured me.

"She was out stemming in front of CVS. I thought I could trust her, but I guess I was wrong. My Sony digital camera, photos ..." he trailed off in disappointment.

When Neal returned to retrieve his cart, Jersey was gone and the cart was nowhere to be found. Neal was sure she had stolen it. Other than that cart and a collection of things he kept at his mother's home, he didn't have anything except a few miscellaneous items stashed in the daylilies on Neal's Island.

"I'm sorry," I said.

Neal took a nap and later I encouraged him to call the police. But Neal said, "They don't care about a homeless person."

A couple of hours later, Neal had a merciful, maybe even indifferent, attitude about his missing cart. "It's just stuff," he said. "And it's a beautiful day. I'm not gonna let that get me down."

It was a good thing he didn't call the police, because a few hours later, Jersey got out of a car in front of CVS. And in the trunk, like precious cargo, was Neal's cart, safe and sound.

This night, although Simon seemed ready for a mission, the reality of *if* and *how* he would find the attackers remained unknown.

"I love you, man," he told me again.

"Love you too, man. Peace," I said.

Simon got up and woke up Neal. They walked around Harvard Square before sunrise, like vigilantes guarding the early frontier, Neal carrying a mallet and some other hand tool, like a police officer with a billy club and gun. Neal warned me, "Every once in a while this happens, John. Punks will go around and beat up homeless people."

At that point, we had only a limited understanding of what had occurred. But when I walked by the Coop, I could see sprinkles of Chet's blood and could retrace some of his steps down the sidewalk from the dried red drops that had fallen from his face.

The rest of the day, Chet lay in the cemetery, hidden in the back where it was private and where you'd have to be looking for him to notice him. There he rested in the grass with a bloody shirt, swollen face, and wounds that were beginning to scab over. I brought him a couple of ice packs from a locker I kept in the library, the kind that get icy when you break up the chemicals inside them.

"You want me to put one on you?" I asked him.

"It ain't no big deal," he said. "I'm alright."

Chet didn't seem particularly humiliated by what had happened. Apparently, around midnight, he had walked down the sidewalk from CVS to the alcove of the Coop to make a drug deal. Chet got his money out, and before he knew it, the two guys he'd agreed to buy crack cocaine from attacked him, bloodied his face, stole his money, and ran away.

Chet seemed to be treating what had happened like the cost of doing business, just a normal thing that could happen on any given day. But down deep — beneath his tough guy personality, beneath his "don't pray for me" mentality — were probably the same thoughts and feelings that you and I would have if something like that happened to us. A couple of days after the assault, Chet and Becky were back to their usual selves, stemming next to CVS. For some reason, they were in an unusually good mood. Perhaps they had received their checks, which I had heard they received every month. They both told me they appreciated my visit to the cemetery and the ice packs I had left behind.

Chubby John said that, for no reason at all, Chet had given him some money. And Becky had bought him cigarettes, despite the fact that she and Chubby John often competed for the CVS stemming spot. Becky smiled and told Chubby John, "We're just like a family. You know families fight, but then we all get along." For the rest of the day, Chubby John was all smiles, impersonating Becky, retelling exactly what she had said and the way she had said it.

Before long, Chet said he was looking for something else to mellow him out. It sounded like his last experience buying drugs wasn't going to deter him from trying again. He'd soon suffer a stroke and would leave Harvard Square in an ambulance. Like so many others, though, he'd return as soon as he could, but with strict doctor's orders to begin eating healthy and to quit smoking and taking drugs.

We heard that the police had caught one of the suspects, but that didn't seem to be what put Chet and Becky in a festive mood. Chet said he wasn't even going to press charges. He preferred revenge, though he didn't seem to consider the difficulty of finding the culprits.

"I never forget a face," he threatened, adding some expletives. "I ain't in no hurry. They messed with the wrong person."

In the words of

CHUBBY JOHN

When you're on the streets, what you need is a safe place. You need a safe shelter to stay at. When you don't have a safe shelter, then you really can't work. You need that home base. How can you go find work when you've just rolled out of a tent? I think what is needed are more safe shelters, like some of the smaller ones in Cambridge. You can get a decent meal, a good night's sleep, and a fresh shower.

When you're homeless, you depend on everyone else. Initially, I thought I could make it on my own. I wasn't going to need any help from anybody. I was going to fix my own problems. I got myself into this situation; I was going to get myself out of it. I didn't need help from anybody. Well, you learn after a few months out there that if you don't ask people for help — and there are people willing to give it — you're never going to make it on your own. I tell people that now on the street.

My theory was that, out on the street, you have to be on your toes. Anything could happen at any time. I wasn't going to be ten sheets to the wind passed out under a tree and getting killed. When I first became homeless, I became depressed and was drinking heavily because I lost everything. And then I realized really quickly that when you're on the street, you really can't be drinking. Nobody on the street ever saw me really drinking. They might have seen me have a beer or two here or there, but nobody ever saw me getting drunk.

I met plenty of good people and great organizations on the street. Starlight Ministries is one of the best organizations I ever met. They're a Christian organization, but they don't jam their Christian beliefs down anyone's throat. They're just there to assist anyone who needs assistance. I support their fundraiser walk every year. That organization actually keeps people alive. They feed you. They give you blankets. And blankets and socks are the two most important things people need on the street.

The federal government needs to step up to make some kind of program to really start stitching up the wounds, because the shelters and all of these other organizations are just band-aids, and the band-aids can only hold on for so long.

I'd like to start some organization like Habitat for Humanity, only the buildings would be for homeless people. And if the homeless help fix up an abandoned property or house that's falling down, then they would get into it. You'd have to work somehow with the federal government to get some subsidy. I think in a ten-year period, you could build a whole lot of buildings and get a lot of people off the street. Someday I'd like to maybe focus on doing something down that road.

A lot of people you run into that give you money or stop and talk or buy you a sandwich have the misconception that every homeless person they encounter is either an alcoholic or a drug addict. Not all homeless people are bad, but you're going to find some people that are always going to be homeless. They're going to be homeless by choice. That's their lifestyle. And you're going to find some people who are just so mentally incompetent that they don't know anything better. You'll find that, yeah, there are a good percentage of alcoholics and drug addicts out there in the homeless world, but there are a great percentage that aren't. They're just people down on their luck, struggling to get themselves back on their feet. Sometimes by just talking to people, you help them realize that not everybody on the street is like that.

John Lithgow, the actor, came walking up to me one day. I'm sitting on the crate and I see this guy. I'm looking at him and thinking, *Boy, this guy looks awfully familiar. Who is this guy?* I'm staring at him as he's walking down the sidewalk. And he sees me staring. So he walks over and says, "Hi, how's it going?"

I said, "It's not going too bad. You know what? I was watching you walk up here, and I just realized who I think you look like. I think you look just like that guy from *Third Rock from the Sun*, John Lithgow."

He laughed, and he said, "You know, I get that all the time." Then he said, "What are we doing here?"

I said, "Oh, I'm trying to get a little help, get some food, whatever I can get."

He said, "Let me see what I can do." And he reached in his wallet and handed me a twenty-dollar bill. He said, "See you later," and walked up the street.

Then, I see people running down the street five minutes later saying, "Hey, did you see John Lithgow? Which way did he go?"

I found out he's on a board at Harvard, and he was actually speaking at Harvard that afternoon. It really was John Lithgow. I didn't realize it at the time. He was nice to me. He helped me out. So you never know who you're going to run into.

Initially, stemming bothered me. You'd be sitting there and people would come by and they'd make every comment in the book that they could about your sitting there. You're this; you're that. You're these; you're those. And it used to irritate me. Initially, I argued with them. Others would say, "Here I got something for you," and they'd toss one penny in the cup. And that used to irritate me too. But I learned, over time, you just smile. These people are going to be miserable in life no matter what they do. So I learned over a period of time, when somebody came by and threw a penny in my cup, I'd say, "Thank you very much. Every penny counts. I greatly appreciate it!" And usually they'd get mad at you as they walked away. And to the people that used to come by and make their mumble-jumble, I'd just say, "God bless you. I'll say a prayer for you tonight." And they'd usually look at you and say, "What's this guy talking about? Is this guy crazy?" You learn not to let them bother you. Because they're just miserable people who have no sympathy for anyone who is down on their luck.

Before I became homeless, I don't think I was as nice of a person. I used to walk by people asking for change and just give them a dirty look and keep walking. I think until you're in their shoes, you don't realize some things. So I think it made me a better person, being out there. I wouldn't change anything. I have no regrets. It made me open my eyes and realize there's good and bad in every walk of life.

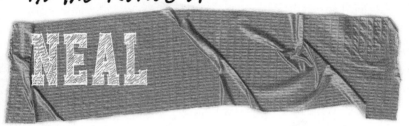

In the words of

NEAL

My dad was an alcoholic. It runs in the family. I pretty much left home when I was fifteen. I hitchhiked across the country by myself, with my backpack and guitar. I just always felt like a black sheep in society, kind of like a square peg in a round hole. I always felt different. And you know something? I heard in Alcoholics Anonymous that most alcoholics feel that way. They feel different. They don't fit. I always assumed I could be a loner. But I cannot. I have to have people to talk to sometimes.

You know something? The few serious relationships I had, those women loved me. They were hardworking. They weren't drunks. And they did everything they could to help me. And I ruined every single relationship. I felt like I wasn't worthy of having a regular life. Now I feel differently, though. Now I feel like when these drunks on the streets come to talk to me, I say, "Excuse me, do you have an appointment?" I feel more important now because my self-esteem is better now than it ever was. I feel more right about what I'm saying. I quit all the bull, and my morals are better.

I feel I've lost the game of life, but I feel like I've also gained more wisdom in my life. I'm not just me anymore. I'm like the poem "Footprints." He's carrying me along. Sometimes I feel like I'm a little heavy.

It's time for me to do something. I can do something. I feel like I've tried so many times to do the right thing, but I've never been able to get it done. Alcohol has pretty much ruined my life. I could've been a doctor. I could've been something. I came up in a family with money. I had the intelligence to do things in my life, and I just threw it away. Now I've got nothing.

This is how I am: Anything that I love to do, I excel at. But I fail at everything that I don't like to do. Some people — really intelligent people — they're good at anything, even if they don't like doing it. I have to like doing it. I won't do anything if I don't like doing it. See, I'm a different kind of person that way. I never went forward.

We all have to live with our demons. I haven't done cocaine in seventeen years. I just walked away from it. Enough is enough. Beer is my only demon. And it doesn't make me evil. I just drink beer. I listen to music. I paint on canvas. The reason I want to get sober is because I don't do anything. I don't play my guitar now. I don't do artwork. You know something? When you don't do anything, it causes depression. You just stare off into space and all you do is get wrapped up in all your thoughts about how crappy your life is. You've got to keep busy.

You know, as a matter of fact, I think somewhere in the Scriptures it says you have to work, and do something. All sloth is doing is ruining you, and God gave us a purpose to do something, not just sit around. You've got to do something. And it's hard, because being an alcoholic is hard, because it's so hard to quit it. I've been drinking since I was fourteen, and I know no other life. I don't know anything else. I've traveled. I had some little jobs here and there. But alcoholism is a disease that keeps getting worse. Even though you don't even notice it, it's happening. One of my friends was just drinking beer all the time, like me, and graduated to vodka. Now, when you see him drink vodka, he gets violent — not against me but against other people. He starts fights. He doesn't even know what he's doing.

If I quit drinking, I'd spend most of my time in the church. I'm not a drunkard in the tabernacle — in the church. I don't get drunk and go in the church. I never get drunk. Beer keeps my blood alcohol level where I'm satisfied. You'll never see me stumbling down the road, like a stumblebum. You'll never see that. You won't see me falling-down-drunk.

I'm fifty-four years old, and I'm medically ill. I need to get a place to live. How hard is that? Just a little room with an electric plug for my TV — that's all I want. I'm getting old. Homelessness is getting old.

That's another thing, though — when I'm inside, sometimes I feel myself watching television, because I love television, entertainment, and movies. After a while, I start getting depressed from just staring at the TV all day, like I have no life at all — except it's a better life than just sitting outside with a beer. It's better to have a TV and be bored and drinking than be sitting with no TV and drinking. But sometimes I feel like it's better to be out here. I'd find myself stuck inside. I'd want to just shut the whole world out. I might become like a recluse or something, if I get a place. I might not come out; I'd just stay in there and play with the little things I own and cook some food and watch my TV. I'm not sure if I would like that.

five

PRAYER IN THE PARK

It was a Saturday morning, and a sign advertising the thrift shop at the Red Doors Church caught my eye. For one of my homeless friends, who was walking with me, the thrift shop was a place to purchase "pee-free clothes." After having spent a couple of weeks in Harvard Square, she claimed that all of her clothes smelled of urine because of where she stashed her belongings during the daytime. I had long been a fan of thrift shops and their many cousins — auctions, yard sales, and used clothing stores — and that morning I imagined all the wonderful, cheap treasures the thrift shop had inside.

Even as a young teenager, I'd scour the classified section of the Friday newspaper, mapping out a plan to hit as many garage sales as I could the next day. My buddy and I would begin our Saturdays early — or at least earlier than most of our other middle school friends — taking off on our bicycles like forty-niners racing to the California gold rush. About the only thing I distinctly remember buying at those sales, though, was an old, pocket-sized gardening book, for a dime.

Although garage saling is a pastime I continue to enjoy, I don't pursue it with as much tenacity as I did in my earlier years. Instead of plotting the ground to cover like a carefully thought-out chess game, I take a more spontaneous approach. If I happen upon a sale that looks worthy of perusing, I'll stop and look around. That's just what I did that Saturday morning, and the sale was a good one. Each item was just twenty-five cents.

"Do you like to read?" my friend asked me, as I stooped to check out a few boxes of books.

"I like having read," I said.

But I wasn't looking for books to read. I started wondering if I could make a few bucks by selling some books to the booksellers in the Square.

So far, I hadn't considered selling books as a way to make money while on the streets. I had tried my hand at picking up soda cans and beer bottles, each of which netted a five-cent refund. But because of my lack of concerted effort, the venture had turned out to be nothing less than a failure.

Collecting bottles and cans had seemed like a reasonable way of making a little extra cash. When I began, I had told Neal that collecting them was my new profession. "I used to do that, years ago," he said, approvingly.

"What's your profession now?" I asked.

"Philosopher," he replied, with a big smile.

What one learns by picking up bottles and cans for a week is that water and juice bottles should also have a deposit, which would make bottle collectors happier, the streets cleaner, and the environment healthier. When I was ready to return my collection of forty beer bottles and cans, I took them to a liquor store near Chubby John's campsite and pushed them into the self-service bottle-return machine, keeping close tabs on the time, knowing that my seven-day subway pass was minutes away from expiring. I collected my two dollars from the cashier and sprinted back to the subway station like a boy about to miss his school bus. Unfortunately, I arrived one minute late, and my recently expired pass wasn't worth the paper it was printed on. I put the two dollars I had just made into the ticket machine. *Easy come, easy go,* I said to myself.

As for the soda cans and bottles, I stashed a bag of them in the bushes, and when I went to add more to it a few weeks later, they were gone. Hopefully someone found them and made a few pennies.

Being a philosopher seemed like a much easier job.

Could selling used books be a better way to net a few dollars? It worked for one homeless couple who operated a used bookstand on the sidewalk in Harvard Square. Every book they sold was two dollars, and their customers loved them.

The main drawback to selling books was that I'd have to lug them around in my backpack until I could sell them. I wasn't too concerned about the risk of losing a dollar, or less, buying a few books at the thrift shop that I might not be able to resell in the Square; it wouldn't really set me back financially. Still, how could I select the right books that booksellers would want to buy from me? Would it just be a failed enterprise?

In the past, I had come up with a handful of entrepreneurial ideas, like the time I thought about selling night crawlers out of our garage as a teenager. We didn't live near a lake or river, but it seemed like a good idea in my teenage mind. Fortunately, I didn't try to pursue that one.

My first pursuit in business was as a child, after my sister moved out of her room to go to college. I transformed her bedroom into a baseball card store, complete with candy and soda. I put a sign on her bedroom door, fixed a plastic electronic alarm to it that I had bought at Walmart, and stocked her empty bookcase with Snickers, Twix, Milky Way bars, and bubble gum. My prices were at market rates, and usually a few cents cheaper than at the nearest convenience store. My card store wasn't exceptionally profitable, but at least it was a place for my friends and me to hang out.

When I became a little older, I mowed lawns and had a gardening business — a moderately successful entrepreneurial pursuit — until I began a full-time job while attending a community college. I tried my hand at a couple of other investments and also attempted to start a gift basket business. But that idea gained me nothing but unused baskets, shampoos, and stuffed animals that I finally gave away to a local charity. It netted me nothing but a five-year-long stream of junk mail.

Surely selling used books would be more successful than that, so I selected three books from the thrift shop at the Red Doors Church: one about C. S. Lewis and Sigmund Freud, the other two a Sherlock Holmes hardback set. *Who wouldn't want Sherlock Holmes?* I thought. I paid one of the workers seventy-five cents and loaded the books in my bag. The result? I sold the book about Lewis and Freud for something like three dollars to a used bookstore in the Square, and I gave away the Sherlock Holmes books. Nobody wanted to buy them.

This same Saturday was the day Neal and I had set to meet in the Common for a prayer meeting and Bible study. A few nights before, I had walked through the Square to find four people, including

Chubby John, Neal, and our friend Spare Change Spencer, who sold the *Spare Change News* newspaper, sitting on the benches near CVS, singing.

"John," Neal said to me, "I've been thinking; we need to do some prayer and meditation, like in the Common. We've been hanging out; we should spend time in prayer and discussing Scripture."

"How long?" I asked, interested.

"A couple hours. I'm retired," Neal responded, in a serious kind of way.

"Do you have a Bible?" I asked.

"Yes. I never don't have a Bible."

So we agreed to have our prayer meeting on Saturday. Our meeting wouldn't be just for Neal's benefit, either. It would be good for me to pray more too; it was something I hadn't done a whole lot of, and that was in need of changing. It would be like a retreat, something we both would look forward to. The Common wasn't exactly a national park, but it seemed like a place where we'd find reasonable quietude away from CVS and the hustle and bustle of Neal's Island, despite its being just a football field's distance away.

We made our pact that night to have our retreat, and walked toward the Common, where Neal wanted to sleep. "I really want to drink less and be in devotion to the Lord Jesus of Nazareth," he told me as we walked.

We saw a police van parked on a nearby street, as if the officer inside was surveying the Common. "They can't do anything to us," Neal insisted. "In Florida, they'll arrest you for being homeless. I got put in jail once, and I asked why, and the cop said, 'Cause you're breathing.'" Neal laughed hysterically at the memory. He'd said just a few days before, "Laughter keeps me alive."

A few yards away from us stood *The Great Hunger* monument,

dedicated by the president of Ireland in 1997, to remember the Irish Potato Famine of the midnineteenth century. The bronze figures, especially the impoverished woman holding her baby, speak a thousand words about poverty. "Never again should a people starve in a world of plenty," the inscription reads.

Neal looked down at the grass, stationed his cart, and chose the spot that would serve as his resting spot. He had no sleeping bag, since he lost it in a recent dispute with somebody who insisted Neal's sleeping bag was really his.

"This isn't any way to live. C'mon," I said to Neal.

"I have my North Face coat on," he said, trying to reassure me. "And where's my blankie that Charlie got me?" He looked for the small blanket that our non-homeless friend, who lived nearby, had recently purchased for him. Finding it in his cart, Neal laid it on the grass, making his bed for the night.

Quite a life it is, I thought.

Just like many of us, Neal had regrets about his life and questions about the future. I don't think Neal *wanted* to drink like he did. He just didn't think he had much of a choice. He seemed to be sensitive to God's desire for his life. Sometimes he'd say things that gave a glimpse into the struggles he had with himself, such as, "Every time I complain that I'm broke, I think about kids with cancer. And I have to apologize to the Lord."

And one time Neal said to me, "We should really be spreading the news of Christ. We talk about it if someone brings it up, but we should be asking people if they know Christ."

I'd later learn that, in his younger years, Neal had considered going into the ministry.

Neal had lots of friends in the homeless community, as well as friends who were not homeless, such as Amy, who after having met us, stopped by often on her bike. Sometimes Neal met Christian visitors who would chat for a while and buy him something to eat.

Although Amy and others had the capacity to support Neal in ways that his street friends couldn't, the atmosphere of street living was difficult. I remember thinking, after my first week on the streets, that I had never heard the f-word more in my life. And normal street talk often included crass conversations and degrading and sexual comments about others. Being around profanity and gaining an insider's view of the street culture affected, to a certain extent, my own thinking and attitude, weighing on me at times. I'd find myself thinking in the voice of someone on the streets or, at times, felt myself agitated with others, no doubt reflecting normal stress I was under at the time.

Sitting on a bench eating pita bread, Neal looked at me once and said, "You know what, John? You're looking like a real bum." Chubby John said I had bags under my eyes. "Pretty soon you'll have luggage," he joked.

The deeper people sink into the pit of despair on the streets — pulled into thinking that the alternative culture of street life is not just legitimate but just right for them — the more their hopes and dreams die for anything different. I think down deep, even people on the streets knew that. "You can see how people lose hope out here and start drinking," Chubby John commented, when he and I were speaking with the pastor of the Outdoor Church one Sunday.

For some, alcohol is an escape from past failures, daily anxieties, or fears of the future. And it can also be complicated by mental illness.

Neal would tell me, just a few weeks later from a hospital bed, that drinking with friends on the streets helped being on the streets.

In my opinion, it was that very element of "help" that, in reality, actually hurt.

I asked Neal what he thought about his drinking in light of his faith. He wanted to stop drinking, but couldn't figure out why he couldn't. "Cause you keep picking it back up," I said, realizing that my comment was insensitive to the difficulties he faced.

"There's nothing that you've said that I don't already know," Neal replied. Then he reminded me that he was a philosopher and could help answer any questions that I had.

My talks with Neal were some of the best experiences of my time on the streets. I probably hid most of my frustrations from him, because that's what we often do when we're around people who do things that we believe are not in their best interests. Maybe I reinvented his drinking habits in my mind, believing that what he did with his life was his own business and would probably go unchanged by my opinions anyway. Just because we didn't agree on everything, though, didn't mean we couldn't be friends.

At some point during the summer, Neal showed me a flat, bluish-gray stone that looked like it had been smoothed in a riverbed. At some point, water or weather had broken it in two. It was a stone you might use for skipping from the shore of a calm lake. He showed the stone to me using both hands, holding the two pieces together like one half wasn't meant to be considered apart from the other. He gave me one of the pieces, told me how our friendship was important to him, and how that little stone symbolized our relationship. I was a part of him, and he was a part of me. To Neal, the rock halves fit together just like friends did.

One day, Neal said to me, "I drink a lot of beer and laugh a lot. But you know, John, I'm really brilliant. And I've been studying you ever since I met you, and I came to the conclusion of what you should become."

Then there was a pause, as if he was still thinking about how to finish his thought or wanted to be sure I was truly interested. I was.

"Are you gonna tell me?"

Using a serious voice, he said, "You should study the Scriptures and become a reverend of a church. And marry a good woman and have children, if you want them."

He assured me he'd help me with the "marry a good woman" part when I suggested he could offer me some assistance. "I know what I'll tell her," he said confidently, thinking of what he would say. "I have a friend whose name is John. He's a good-looking guy, and he'd like to meet a woman. I'll set you up on a blind date."

Despite our differences, I had felt that Neal and I shared something in common: a desire to have someone to love forever, and be forever loved by. Whether I already knew my future wife or had yet to meet her, my desire was that I be with the right one for me. My guess was that Neal had a similar hope for himself. Despite what Neal had told me about not wanting to marry again, I thought that down deep, he desired the same thing I did.

Throughout the summer, he'd say things such as, "Relationships are based on friendship; you must be best friends first." Neal seemed to be pretty good at sharing advice, if you asked for it. He was also good at sharing what he believed about God, yet he was careful to say that he could not know what God knew.

"You just have to trust that God will bring her to you," he told me once, like a pastor counseling a parishioner.

"I don't necessarily believe that," I responded. "I believe it's up to me."

Over the years, as a result of theological quandaries, conversations, and some jadedness, I had switched from believing that God had complete authority over such matters, to thinking that maybe finding my wife was more of my own responsibility. I also believed that it could be a little bit of both. I didn't know it then, but true to Neal's counsel, the way I'd meet my wife one year later would help me understand God's providence in a new way.

"I know, John. But God can bring her to you," Neal assured me. "She might trip in front of you and you help her up or something."

And that's almost exactly what happened the very next summer. One year after our conversation, as my holiday was nearing its end, I was searching for a particular kind of carpet in Jerusalem. I'd spent some time there after traveling to the region when given the opportunity to visit parts of Abraham's Path in Palestine. I was seconds away from buying a bright green carpet when I saw that they were all made in Turkey, where I'd planned to travel next before returning home. Immediately, the thought came into my mind, *I'll wait until I get to Turkey to buy one.*

A few weeks later, as I carefully assessed the carpets at a souvenir shop in Istanbul, a young woman was perusing scarves behind me, passing time while awaiting her friend, who was running late for dinner. Thinking that I worked at the shop, and considering purchasing a carpet herself, she asked me their prices, in Turkish. I turned around and, not knowing any Turkish, answered her. Then I asked her to pick a carpet out for me, and she asked me to pick one out for her. A little while later, she, her friend, and I had a picnic nearby, and less than four months later, we decided to get married. Now we have two carpets.

It was just like Neal had said. "God can bring her to you."

I waited in the Common for Neal, looking forward to our Saturday prayer retreat. Neal had been feeling ill, but came to find me late in the morning near CVS. "It's 10:55," he said, promising that we'd begin soon. He wanted to check out the thrift shop before it closed.

For Neal, the thrift shop was full of new treasures he could add to his collection of knickknacks. Others we knew had had successful shopping trips there as well. Spare Change Spencer had bought some clothes, and Chubby John had bought a pair of shorts for swimming in the ocean.

After he was finished shopping, Neal came to the Common, where I awaited him. He was carrying a huge black duffle bag and was as happy as if it were filled with ten-dollar bills. "I got you a fun gift and a serious gift," Neal told me, as he sat down. He gave me a wooden spinning top toy with four Hebrew letters painted in bright colors that spelled the word *shalom*. "That's the fun gift," Neal said. The serious gift was a cherry-colored wooden box. Neal admired it so much, though, that I wanted him to keep it. Little boxes were probably his favorite things to collect.

Neal's twenty-five cent purchases also included a little painting, a photo album, an extra-large clothespin, shirts, a metal file, an antique barbell, black art paper, and a green laptop bag imprinted with some company's logo. "I can do white chalk drawings now," he said, pointing to the black paper. "And I'll put my art supplies in here," he said, holding up the laptop bag.

After he showed me his new purchases, Neal and I started to pray. "Thank you, Lord, for the sunshine," Neal prayed, "for friends, life, another day to live. Lord, please help those who are mentally ill, people who don't want to live, those who are going through rough times. Give them sunshine and happiness. Jesus, you know I'm sick. I'll try to do better, eat healthier, get more exercise, try not to drink as much, cause I know you're not crazy about that."

After he was finished, I quietly sang an old hymn and said a prayer. But our retreat wasn't quiet for too long. Jared came by and I asked him if there was anything we could pray about for him.

"Enough fuel in hell for when I get there," he said.

six

THE IN CROWD

You never know what might happen when you're sleeping in a park such as the Common. On windy nights, cold gusts wake you. Skunks prowl around. You never know if the place you bed down is completely dry — or clean, for that matter. And of course, people walk by, cause trouble nearby, or just sleep nearby.

One morning, a stranger with a cut around his eye arose from the granite bench that Spare Change Spencer normally used as a bed. "You know where a Western Union is?" he asked me. I told him the location of a nearby bank, trying to be as helpful as I could. "I was supposed to stay with my friend in Salem, but he got arrested," the man said. "I lost my cell phone," he added. Then, pointing to a cigarette one of my homeless friends held, he asked, "I don't mean to be rude, but you have an extra one of those?"

Chubby John had been standing nearby, and after the man left us, he walked over. "That guy's a detective. Why's he over here? I've seen him in the Harvard office building. Every once in a while something will happen and they'll all come down. They wear suits and have their badges around their necks."

It did seem a bit strange, a detective sleeping in the Common. I told Chubby John what the man had said, that he had what looked like an injury to his eye, and that he'd asked our friend for a cigarette, but not me.

"That's probably cause he knows everything about you and knows you don't smoke or drink," Chubby John assured me. It reminded me of something else Chubby John had once said: "The cops out here know everything about you."

"Every once in a while at this time of year," Chubby John continued, "Harvard does some strange things. They'll send out detectives and bring them in from other states to see what's going on out here."

Maybe the man was a detective. Maybe the mark on his eye was just part of his everyday-man's getup. In a way, what Chubby John said made sense. Homeless people have resided around Harvard for many years, and sometimes they've been deemed troublemakers. As early as 1685, a man with "no settled abode" was found guilty of "disorderly living" and corrupting the manners of the local scholars.* It was now nearing a new school year, and there had been some trouble on the streets, including an episode with Please Leave Larry, who slept in another part of the Common. He had supposedly flashed a badge at a woman and her granddaughter as they walked through the Common. Why he did it, or whether it was true, I don't know. Another problem involved some tents that had supposedly been stolen from Harvard's campus. Word on the street was that a local drug dealer, earlier in the summer, had snatched them after a Harvard group had used them on a camping trip. Coincidently, I had recently informed a Harvard police officer that a tent — maybe one of Harvard's — had shown up in the Common and that it might

* William E. Nelson, *The Common Law in Colonial America*, vol. 1, *The Chesapeake and New England, 1607 – 1660* (New York: Oxford Univ. Press, 2008), 51.

belong to the university. I sometimes used it as a giant polyester and nylon blanket to cover me on nights when the wind was strong.

A part of me — the part that liked to imagine police spies looking out for my protection and the protection of students moving onto campus — believed the man was a detective. But the other part — the realistic one — told me that he probably wasn't. I mean, was there enough going on around the Square to justify spending resources to station undercover police officers — especially ones from other states — to check up on the local homeless population?

Well, maybe there was.

We didn't know it then, but we'd soon learn that Spare Change Spencer, on the very bench on which we'd found the stranger sleeping, had had an altercation that night. Two guys woke him up at 1:55 a.m., asking him for a cigarette lighter so they could smoke crack. Spare Change Spencer not only didn't like being awakened in the night to be asked for a lighter; he didn't want them smoking crack next to him either. They exchanged words. The two guys pulled out a knife, and Spare Change Spencer left to find a safer sleeping spot.

Although I had been sleeping on the grass just a few feet away from him, I had not heard any of it, no doubt because I had taken a dose of an over-the-counter sleeping aid before turning in for the night. Spare Change Spencer was worked up all that next day and told the story again and again.

That next evening, he said to me in a serious voice that sounded like a cross between warning and scolding, "Don't take this the wrong way, but I need to tell you somethin'. Don't take any more sleepin' pills. What happened last night, there shoulda been people who jumped up after hearin' that. This ain't home."

I told Spare Change Spencer that I didn't take the sleeping aid every night, but defended my right to take it. I pointed out how some people did what they felt they had to do to survive on the streets and get a good night's rest: popping black market prescription pills or drinking alcohol. But Spare Change Spencer was right. Our collective safety was more important.

Maybe it was fortuity that a detective happened to come in the Common at a time when danger had been imminent — for all of us. Or maybe it was just a coincidence that the man resembled a local detective that Chubby John had seen before. Whoever he was, I never saw him again. And that's the way it was in Harvard Square. People would come, and people would go.

Since that first night I slept in the Coop and met Teresa, she had visited Harvard Square periodically. Neal had taken her to the theater to see *My Sister's Keeper*, but then he stopped talking to her because he claimed she was too mentally ill. Teresa was often a loner. She usually called me someone else's name and, probably because of her size, was sometimes the subject of foul put-downs, like those you might have heard in high school. Teresa stayed around for only a couple of weeks after I met her.

One night, during the street party when Hank gave me half of his hamburger, Teresa hugged me, said goodbye, and told me she was going to Seattle the next day on a three-day bus ride. She had obtained financial assistance from an organization to help her get there, but she didn't seem to have a place to go once she arrived.

Usually, when someone leaves Harvard Square, it is uneventful, but after Teresa left, everyone around CVS was claiming that *she* was really a *he*.

"Her name was probably Terence, not Teresa," Jared said.

Chubby John said he thought she was a man all along, because of her Adam's apple.

Dane declared, "I know a guy from the pit who knows for a fact that Teresa is a man."

"I could tell by lookin' at her," somebody else said. "She was bigger than me."

"Why do you think she wore so much lipstick?" Jared asked.

Neal and I doubted the rumor. "I saw pictures of her as a little girl," Neal said, remembering that first night we had seen her stemming, holding a picture of her and Santa Claus. It seemed like Neal and I — like older children holding onto faith in the tooth fairy — were the only believers.

Maybe Teresa was a man, or maybe she wasn't. It didn't matter. What did matter is how she — or her memory, rather — was treated. Perhaps Teresa had atypical sexual characteristics. Perhaps she was an intersexed or ambiguously gendered person living in an era when individuals who don't conform to society's notions of gender identity are ostracized. Whatever the case, the ordeal was another testament to what Neal had always called Harvard Square's "ridiculousness."

You never knew what might happen on any given day in front of CVS. Sometimes something meaningful or heartwarming happened, like a conversation Chubby John told us he'd had with four young teenage boys outside CVS when he was stemming one evening. I always enjoyed hearing Chubby John tell stories, and this time he recounted how one of the four boys had stayed outside to watch his and his friends' bicycles while the others went inside CVS. John offered to watch the bikes so the lone boy could join his friends inside the store. The boy accepted John's offer, went inside, and when he came back out, he said to his friends, who were now waiting for him, "I'm a nickel short." John quickly picked out a nickel from his stemming cup and gave it to the boy.

"Don't you need the money?" the surprised boy asked John.

"I don't need it that bad," John said. "It's just a nickel."

The boy took the nickel and went back inside the store to make his purchase. After he came back out, the boy asked Chubby John, "Why did you give me the money?"

John took the inquiry as an opportunity to give all the boys a little lesson about the homeless, along with some personal encouragement to motivate them to succeed in life.

"We're not all bad people," he said to the boys.

Giving the young teens some advice, he encouraged them to get an education so that they wouldn't be out asking for money themselves someday. Chubby John said that the boys listened intently, and then talked among themselves. Before they left, they dug into their pockets and dropped into his cup about a dollar fifty in coins. That nickel and brief conversation had repaid John many times over, and probably instilled in those boys an important lesson.

Dramas, big and small, also took place around Harvard Square, like movies on cable TV. One afternoon, Dane came by excited that he had just found a camera at the local cafe. Immediately, like a man selling Rolex watches from the inside of a long dark coat, Dane put it up for sale. The camera was passed around as the story came out how Dane had acquired it — taking it off a table after its previous owners left.

I challenged Dane to do what I believed to be the right thing — turn it in to the cafe's management as lost property.

"That's not putting any money in my pocket," Dane countered.

I tried to reason with him. "The people might come back looking for it. How would you feel if you lost your camera and somebody took it?"

It was no use. Dane didn't want the previous owners' emotions disturbing his potential profit.

I felt frustrated at Dane's insensitivity for not considering others before himself. That was my perception, though, as an outsider in a culture often focused more on self and survival than neighbor and altruism. Dane didn't think his actions equated to the kinds of thefts that he committed when he was on cocaine. Maybe I'm wrong, but I think what he did still came pretty close.

Most of the time, life was normal — as normal as it could be for people living on the streets. Dane told me the evening I stemmed in traffic that I should, to use his words, enjoy "sitting back, being with friends, staying warm and dry." Neal seconded that. Neither of them, though, were stamping blue ribbons of approval on their way of living. They weren't advocating the homeless lifestyle as the model for a flourishing life. Rather, they seemed to be making the best of the situations they were in. They knew how to live, despite their circumstances. People on the streets could, at least sometimes, support each other, knowing that being together was better than being alone.

It was probably Jared's talk about the Millionaire's Ring that inspired Neal to start talking about forming his own group, the In Crowd. He'd sing, "I'm in with the in crowd; I go where the in crowd goes." One day, he announced to his friend James and me that he was about to initiate a new club — a movement, he called it — the In Crowd Movement.

"There will be rules," Neal informed us. "Like no lying. And there will be signatures," he said, explaining how each new member — who joined by invitation only — would sign and warrant that he or she would abide by the rules of the In Crowd.

It sounded like Neal's club already had an advantage over Jared's Millionaire's Ring, which didn't have any organization to it. The Millionaire's Ring was just a name Jared arbitrarily assigned to any group of homeless people he'd see. "There's the Millionaire's Ring," he'd say, to any group of two or more homeless people he knew. At least with the In Crowd, comprised of people who enjoyed spending time together, there'd be formality and accountability.

I'm sure Neal already had in mind who would be in his club. James would have been in the In Crowd, because they were planning to be roommates soon. "We're gonna have so much fun," Neal said, dreaming about living indoors with James. For sure, Amy would be at the top of the membership list. She visited regularly, Neal had bought her a Curious George stuffed animal, and she kept us apprised of her summer travel plans, which sometimes made Neal sad, because he knew that meant she'd be leaving for a while. Amy was definitely a shoo-in for the In Crowd.

One of our evenings together — with Chubby John, Amy, Spare Change Spencer, and me looking on — Neal wanted to prove the truth of a simple statement I had made that he owned Harvard Square. He stood up from the brick sidewalk and proceeded to lay, face down, upon it. As Neal's nose neared the sidewalk, the brim of his red cap touched the bricks and tipped off his head. His long body lay straight for a few moments as he enjoyed our attention. I think he did it just to show us that he would — or could — lie pros-trate in the middle of the sidewalk. He proved, in a way, that he felt the freedom to do so in a place where he had spent many years. "My mother started bringing me down here when I was five years old," Neal said, as he stood up, proud of his nearly a half-century's experience in the Square.

I had passed out all of the remaining snacks left over from my class that night — something my Harvard friends always asked me to do — and we were enjoying being together on a warm summer evening. But Neal wouldn't have said that everyone who stopped by that evening was a friend.

I don't know who it was, but someone came by and thanked Neal for giving him a drink of beer at some earlier time. He said Neal had also taken a drink from his bottle. While I had thought the man was just being appreciative, Neal knew the man wanted something. Neal didn't know the stranger, hadn't drunk from his bottle, and didn't appreciate anyone trying to trick him. "When you're out on the streets, you've got to take care of yourself," Neal poignantly told me after the man left. He was visibly agitated and convinced that the man had lied to him in the hopes that Neal would let him drink some of his beer. "Don't be asking me for booze and stuff," Neal stated, as if the stranger were still in our midst. "If you ask me for food, that's another thing. I'll do what I can."

Not everyone got along well in Harvard Square, but there was a sense of community among many. This might have been because of commonalities some had with others, or because homeless people may have felt that other homeless people were their neighbors.

As the summer progressed, Chubby John began sleeping in the Common sometimes so he could wake up by four or five o'clock in the morning to grab the coveted stemming spot outside CVS.

Every so often, somebody would kick over his cup or say out loud, "I hate these scummy bums." But the greetings and generosity of CVS customers and other passersby generally outweighed Chubby John's report of any negative things that happened during the day. After that time of stemming in traffic with Neal and Dane, I never wanted to hold a cup unless it had something cold or hot to drink in it. But on a couple of occasions, I got roped into stemming again.

One day, Graham, the non-homeless man with whom Hank stayed, wanted me to hold the spot where he often stemmed while he went home for an hour. At first, I declined; I didn't like the idea of stemming by myself. Chubby John, who was stemming in front of CVS, a couple of stores down from Graham, and had heard our conversation, encouraged me to accept Graham's offer. "You should do it to learn how it's really like for people who are out here stemming," he told me. "You could get the real experience. Plus, it's lunchtime," he added, noting that it would be a good time to stem.

So to do Graham a favor and to get more of the experience that Chubby John advocated, I accepted. One of our other homeless friends, standing nearby, spoke some encouraging words with a smile and put a dollar into the cup Graham had given me. "This will help you get started," he said.

I walked to a curious brick fixture that looked like a two-foot-tall chimney sticking out of the sidewalk and sat down. I quickly realized that I had sat on blue chewing gum — about as much fun as getting pooped on by a bird, which happened to me twice that summer. Actually, the bird missed each time, hitting my backpack once and, another time, the *Spare Change News* newspaper that I had bought from Spare Change Spencer.

I looked up at the large digital clock atop one of the tallest buildings in the Square. It showed 11:51. I wondered how long the hour would feel. I looked at it again, and it was 11:54.

I was there to hold Graham's stemming spot, though his actual spot was in front of me a few yards. In Harvard Square, stemming etiquette says that people stemming should be either out of sight of other stemmers or far enough away so as not to encroach on another's income. So even though I wasn't at the exact spot on the sidewalk where Graham had been, I was close enough to hold his spot.

Pretty soon, Chet saw me as he came out of the liquor store. With uncharacteristic gusto he said, "I never seen a college student out here with a cup. And you know, you deserve it. I've never given to a college student. I don't want to give up this opportunity!" Then he dug into a pocket in his jeans, saying, "I don't know how much change I got," pulled out four dimes, and dropped them into my cup. It was another week before he was assaulted and I visited him in the cemetery, so his forty-cent gift wasn't a token of gratitude. He seemed to do it for his own amusement.

I heard once that people get used to panhandling. Perhaps it's true for those who've done it for a long time or have made it part of their lifestyle, to survive or perhaps satisfy an addiction. Stemming was always different for me than for others who had, or chose, to do it to sustain themselves or their habits. I could justify being out there to do a favor for Graham or, as Chubby John suggested, to learn firsthand about the experiences of the homeless. Others stem because they feel they have to.

After an hour and nineteen minutes — nineteen minutes more than I had agreed to — I realized that Graham wasn't going to return to his spot, and I was ready to leave. I admit I hadn't tried very hard to make any money while stemming that day. I had hung my head — embarrassed — and looked down, finding distractions in the bricks of the sidewalk and the insects that used them as giant roads. Then I stared into my nearly empty cup. The odd brick fixture I was using as my chair was constructed in a way that I could only half-sit on it, and I felt I was a little distance away from some of the people walking down the sidewalk.

My income that day was $1.40. And it came from two homeless men, who gave it without my asking.

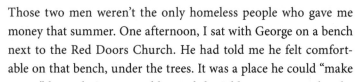

Those two men weren't the only homeless people who gave me money that summer. One afternoon, I sat with George on a bench next to the Red Doors Church. He had told me he felt comfortable on that bench, under the trees. It was a place he could "make peace," he said. George said he read the Bible sometimes when he felt depressed, and enjoyed serving as the church's unofficial watchman. "Two hours volunteering at the church is two hours I'm not drinkin'," he had said.

George was listening to his portable radio, one of his favorite things to do while sitting on that bench. He shared with me some of his cookies and asked if I wanted a beer, although he knew I would decline. Then, all of a sudden, George stood up, fished down into his pocket, and pulled out a ten-dollar bill. "Here, put this in your pocket," he said, handing it to me.

"No, you don't have to give me anything," I said, surprised.

"I know I don't have to; I want you to have it," George said, obstinately. "I'll just drink it up. You'll put it to better use."

Although I had known George for only ten months, it seemed we'd gone way back. I had visited him a couple of times in the hospital the previous fall, and he was always open with me. He supported my interest in learning about homelessness and the people who lived on the streets, and shared with me some things about his life. He admitted to being an alcoholic and told me he'd spent some time in prison.

George's arthritis often bothered him, and he said it was aggravated by sleeping on the ground; he felt that moisture moved into his joints, causing his body to ache more. Fortunately, for most of the summer, George had a place to stay. When he did sleep outside, it was usually on the porch of the Red Doors Church. From what George had told me, his state of homelessness had been off and on for a long time — intermittent but persistent.

After I met George the first time, the day after I first moved to Cambridge, he never forgot my name. One month after I met him, I went with some graduate students to the Red Doors Church to help with their free weekly meal. But when I arrived at the church with my fellow colleagues and talked with the person in charge about my interest in learning more about homelessness, the leader assured me they had enough volunteers for the evening and invited me to take a seat next to someone whom I could learn a lot from. That person was George. As a result, rather than helping serve at the dinner, I was among those being served.

I wanted to be able to apply my interest in homelessness to my studies in my classes, and George was the first to teach me about the ins and outs of homelessness in Harvard Square, as well as the relational bonds between homeless people. A couple of months after we first met, George and I arranged to meet at 6:30 a.m. on a Saturday morning so that I could meet some of his friends and see homelessness the way he had lived it off and on for thirty years.

One of the places George took me was a parking lot in back of a Cambridge Chinese restaurant. It was there that the Breakfast Club used to meet each day, as faithful as postal workers who deliver the mail. The Breakfast Club was a group of five homeless men who sat together, drinking beer, smoking, listening to the radio, and chatting in a street vernacular replete with expletives. They invited me to sit down on an old upside-down bucket, as well as to relieve myself, if I wished, in their makeshift toilet — a bucket that they regularly emptied and cleaned with detergent, wedged between a large building and a shed. I met the president and vice president of the Breakfast Club and learned that George held a titled position as well. No one seemed to mind that it was a cool November day and that it would have been warmer to sit indoors. For the Breakfast Club, though, an indoor venue was probably not an option, at least if smoking, drinking, listening to the radio, and talking the way they did was part of the deal.

When George introduced me to his homeless friends, he told each one of them that I was a Harvard student who was interested in learning more about homelessness. Learning about street life and relationships among the homeless, I began developing an understanding of the theology of relational care, thinking about how relationships between homeless and non-homeless people — specifically Christians — could bring support to those on the streets. That day with George, my eyes were opened to the alternative culture that had formed among their homeless community. I learned how important those guys were to each other, and how they enjoyed being in each other's company. George had even known some of his friends since the 1960s, when they lived together in a tent community along the train tracks.

"It's a lot different out here on the streets than not being on the streets, huh?" I asked him that morning.

"Oh, yeah, it's a whole different world."

George told me all kinds of things about that world that I never would have dreamed of asking, and offered bits of wisdom, like the importance of saying "good morning" and talking to strangers. "If more people walked around with smiles on their faces," he said, "there'd be a lot less hostility in the world."

Occasionally during that summer I spent on the streets, George encouraged me to study so that I would pass my language requirement and graduate. Because I didn't have definitive plans for after the summer, he cautioned me with care, "Don't let the streets grab your butt. It's too easy to stay out here. I've seen a lot of good people just stay on the street."

I wasn't planning for that to happen, though. My intentions were to be off the streets by the end of the summer, and by then, some of my homeless friends would have places of their own too.

GEORGE

I'm Catholic by birth, but my church is really the Red Doors — Christ Church. I've been helping there over thirty years, volunteering. I've only been to a service there twice in the thirty years I've been out here. I go in and say prayers now and then when something's on my mind. But if something's on my mind and I'm walking by another church, I'll go in and say a prayer in there.

Protestant, Muslim, whatever, it doesn't bother me — religion. Everyone has their own faith, and I just follow what I believe. I made my communion and confirmation, and all that — which makes parents happy. I don't practice it. There's no particular reason why. I really never gave it much thought because, after confirmation, now I don't have to do it anymore. I hate being told what to do. I cannot stand that. The more you tell me not to do something, the more I want to do it.

I started picking up drinking when I was about eleven years old. Alcohol made my life worse, and I ended up out on the streets from it. If I could go back, I'd never have screwed up in the first place. I quit high school when I hit the streets in the tenth grade. My father and mother were shocked when I got a double promotion from the eighth to the tenth grade. My father inquired about it. I said, "I didn't get a double promotion; it's just that they didn't wanna put up with me for another year in junior high." My father realized that I wasn't going to be educated. But Mom and Dad were happy that I got a GED. I always wanted to finish. I did something while I was in jail; I didn't just sit back and do nothing. I read a lot. The only time I really read is when I'm locked up.

Life's changed now. I'm working. I'm hoping to get a car by the end of the summer and do a little traveling in the winter. I'm too old for the old stuff anymore. I'm fifty-four years old now. I'm not getting any younger. And I don't want this life — the streets — anymore. I wish my mother was still alive to see how far I came.

In the words of

DANE

*W*hen I took that camera from the cafe, John confronted me as though he were just asking a question. But I felt like he was making a point. And he said, "Um, so that belongs to someone else. They inadvertently left it on the table. So you just took it?"

And I said, "Well, if I didn't take it, someone else was gonna."

And he said, "Yeah, but maybe whoever owned it would come back and find it before that happened."

And I said, "Oh well. I need money."

John was like one of those people that said, "Hey, Dane, look what you're doing."

And I'm like, "Yeah, yeah, yeah, I know. But I'm doing it anyway." I remember that moment. He was the only one that got in my face about that, in a very innocuous way. It wasn't aggressive or assertive; it was just there.

What John was letting me know, without saying it, was, "Dane, that may sit well with you, but not with me." That's what he was really showing me without actually saying it. Which is a good way to say to someone, "Hey, look at yourself for a moment. Just look what you've become, what you're doing. Is that what you should be doing?"

I was like, Who cares? I live in the moment. I just want this. I want this because this represents fifty dollars. And fifty dollars will buy me some pot and some food, and so I'm off on a mission serving Dane.

I had to put that to rest. I couldn't continue like that. I don't do things like that today. When I first moved into my place three years ago, I stole something in the convenience store across the street. The owner has cameras, and he saw me put something in my pocket as I was walking down one of the aisles. And when I came up with my items for purchase, he reached under the counter and he said, "Here," and he put up an identical can of the thing that I had taken. "You can put this with the one in your pocket. Apparently you need it desperately." He said to me, "Sir, if you need something, you can ask me; I will give it to you. You do not have to steal here."

And after that, we became friends. Good friends. He started giving me a line of credit. I can go in and get five or ten dollars' worth of stuff when I don't have the money and pay him the next day or the day after. He helped me. I said, "Sir, I want to tell you that that is not the kind of response that I am accustomed to getting from people when they catch me doing wrong." I said, "The way in which you presented my actions back to me initiated the beginning of a change in me."

And he said to me, "I watch you, but God watches us both." And later, he gave me a little hand-carved statue of a deity from the Hindu belief.

I have like an eleven-page police history. I was incarcerated in county facilities nine times. I was incarcerated in a federal facility once, and the state system twice, over forty-five years of criminal history. Now, I am not wanted by the law.

In terms of that camera, to a guy like John, according to his upbringing, he needs a moment of adjustment to try to understand how someone would not be of the first mind to seek to get the camera back to its rightful owner. I, however, saw it immediately as a golden opportunity. I didn't see it as someone else's loss but as my gain, almost as if it were ordained — a gift from God. I'm homeless. I have no money. It's not even justification, because I don't have to go through the justification process. Right from the outset it's there — opportunity. Without a thought about the person who'd lost it, their loss is my gain, because of the way I was brought up.

Let me begin at the beginning. My mother gave birth to me when she was sixteen years old. My first recollection was of being raised by my grandmother and my uncle Jerry. My mother and father already divorced. My father was off into another marriage with a woman who already had two children. And they had two more. And my mother was up in Boston and she had started another family. So here we were at Nana's, and we were pretty much a burden, and we felt it. We were a duty and a task. And I remember when my nana passed away, we were being ultimately shuttled up to Boston to my mother's new life. But there was a week in between when we were sent over to my father's house. For the weekend that we were there, he never spoke to us, and I remember saying to my brother, "If he's our father, why doesn't he talk to us?"

When we got to our mother's place in Boston, we were kind of treated like second-class citizens. My mother actually referred to us as "the freeloaders," and I remember saying to my brother, "We didn't ask to be born."

I ran away from home one time and hitchhiked to try to connect with my father. I was sixteen. But by the time I got there, I found out that he had died. He and his dog had drowned in a boating accident. Ultimately, I sussed out over the years that he really wanted nothing to do with anything that reminded him of my mother. And I didn't know why until I discovered later that my father had divorced my mother on the grounds of adultery. I believe that the reason that he didn't even acknowledge us when we were in his presence was because he probably went on to have a lifelong question of paternity. My mother had a problem with faithfulness all her life, and she made me a part of that secrecy. It was something heavy to lay on a young child.

I was kind of "assistant mother"; I was the oldest. I learned cooking and ironing and sewing and babies. My mother always had one in her belly, one in her arms, and one on the floor. I have fourteen siblings by three different fathers.

My mother would send me to the door when bill collectors would be knocking, and she would whisper to me what to say: "I sent the check in the mail." I know she didn't, so I'm lying to this guy. But it's okay because there's no police there, and my mother is the one sanctioning it. And we would go shopping, and now and then I'd see my mother nick something and put it in her bag or put it in her pocket. And I would be thinking, *Ma, are you gonna pay for that?* But then I would think, *I better not say that*. So when I wanted something, or when I was in a jam, I just lied, and I just stole, because I learned it from my mom.

But I knew it was wrong.

And then my stepfather would go out to drive cab at night, and my mother had a boyfriend, and I would mind the house, and I couldn't tell my stepfather. I had to keep that secret. And that was hard for me because he was my stepfather, but he was my good friend. He was good to me. He wouldn't say, "That's my stepson." He treated me like his son, and I had to hide what I knew from him. And I became that good phony. That good fake face. That good actor.

My stepfather loved having a family and a wife, and he just didn't ask questions, if he had any thoughts. He just carried on and took care of all the kids. He drove cab all night and went to bed at five in the morning. But if I was in trouble with the law, he'd stay up, and he'd show up in court at nine o'clock. And they'd call my name, and before any lawyers could talk, he'd go up to the judge with his hat in his hand, and start talking to the judge, "Listen, he's getting involved with these bad kids. I'm gonna kick his butt. I got a job for him pumping gas, Your Honor. I'm gonna whip him into shape; he's a good kid." And every time, he'd talk me out of there. And you know, when we'd leave the courthouse, he wouldn't kick my butt or bawl me out; he'd say to me, "Are you hungry?"

And I'd say, "Yeah."

And he'd say, "Let's go get some breakfast." And he'd put his arm around me and that would be it. There'd be no more talk about the court. He was a good man. My mother was his first and only marriage. He drove taxi for forty-seven years in Boston. And I drove taxi for twenty-seven years after him.

In the words of **NEAL**

I love to laugh. So when we're just sitting around drinking a beer or something, and playing trivia games and laughing, that's basically all the fun I have right now in my life. And when people come around with their street dramas — "This guy owes me twenty dollars; I'm gonna kill him; blah, blah, blah" — I'm like, "I don't want to hear it."

I try to stay happy, but someone always ruins it. You know what one of my favorite things to do is? When I wake up in the morning, I go, *Let's see how long it takes before I meet the first person who tries to ruin my day.* Sometimes it's minutes. Sometimes it's an hour. Someone always has to ruin my day, every day. I want to have the day go *la-di-da, what a wonderful day* all the time. I have enough problems with my medical issues and sometimes depression. And I don't want to hear all the negativity. It bores me. On the streets, there's no culture or any kind of interesting conversation. Once in a while, certain people I know — homeless guys — are fun to talk to. My eyes light up when they show up.

Homeless people come around me asking me for money. If somebody comes up and says, "Hey, Neal," in my head I'm thinking,

What does he want? They ask you for something every five minutes. "Got a beer? Got a dollar? Got a cigarette? Got a beer? Got a dollar? Got a cigarette?" It's constant. As a matter of fact, people are so shallow they'll wake up out of their sleeping bag and, without a "good morning" or anything, they'll just say, "Got a cigarette?" They have no concept of regular human behavior. They just get up and go, "Give me." "Give me" is their forte. Always. It never ends. No one ever comes over and goes, "Hey, Neal, look what I got you." No one ever. They always come over and go, "What do you have for me?"

There's always a catch to "Hello, Neal."

So I invented this club. It's called the No Club. I've got three members. And it's kind of a joke, but it's kind of serious too. Even before people walk up to me, I go, "No."

"Can I have a — "

"No."

"Don't I know you from — "

"No."

Everything is no. Before they even talk to you, you know they're going to try to bum something off you. So *no* is kind of a sacred word in the No Club. It takes a lot of guts to say no. A lot of people don't say no in life because they feel like if they say no, you won't like them. But it's the opposite. When you say no to people, they respect you. If you say yes to everybody, they lose respect for you. After you get the hang of saying no, you start to embrace the word.

I first started out with the Give Me Club. Then I graduated to the No Club.

With the Give Me Club, when people come over and ask for something, you go, "Give *you*? No, I'm president of the Give Me Club. Give *me*. You give me, not me give you." Hey, what can I say? I'm the Give Me Club president. It's only stupid to the people that bum off everybody.

You know what my mother always says to me? She goes, "Neal,

don't you understand there's a reason why they're homeless? They're drug addicts, drunks, mentally ill. There's some reason why they're out there living on the street."

And I don't believe her. There must be somebody out there who's an honorable person. But there are none. They're all full of it. They go, "Oh, we're gonna do this, man. We're gonna do that." I'm like, "Okay, let's do it." And they never come through.

So now I don't trust any homeless person. They don't respect their friendship with me. They just go, "Oh, it's just Neal." I hate that.

Friendship and trust are always earned.

Jesus taught me that if somebody asks me for a piece of bread, I have to give it to him. But I'm not responsible for other people's addictions. I try not to deny food; I have trouble denying them food. Everything else, you're on your own. And if somebody comes and asks me for advice, I'll sit and talk to them for two hours and tell them about Jesus.

seven

DIVINITY DIALOGUE

Maybe it was just because I was interested in theology that Bernard asked me questions that he seemed to have been thinking about his whole life. Despite his staunch atheism, or maybe because of it, theological quandaries swirled in his mind like bees around a Coca-Cola bottle on a summer afternoon.

"How do you even know that there is a God?" he asked me the second or third time I met him, months before the summer began. "To me it just doesn't make sense, this thing about God. Say there are two families praying for their sick kids. One child gets healed. 'It's God's will,' they say. The other child dies. 'It's God's will,' they say. They both say it's God's will! How can it be God's will that one child dies and God's will that the other child lives?"

"Well, I don't say that," I replied. "Sometimes bad things just happen. And God is there with us, crying with those of us who've lost somebody. I think bad things like death, cancer, and earthquakes started happening when sin entered into the world. God made a perfect world and didn't want anything to disrupt that perfection. Then sin entered, and the world order turned upside down.

But it doesn't mean God likes it or wants it," I said. It was at least one way of looking at the matter.

"Why did God create the world with sin?" Bernard followed up.

"People messed it up," I said. "God made the world and it was good. People are responsible for changing God's perfect world."

"Well, why would God make a world knowing that people were going to sin?" Bernard asked. "He knew they'd sin."

"I don't know if he knew that," I said. "I don't know what God knows."

"Well then he ain't God," Bernard contended. "God's supposed to be all-knowing. God ain't God if he didn't know."

"But God didn't want to make a world full of puppets, where we say and do everything just like God wants," I responded. "It would be like that if we didn't have a choice. God made us as free people. We're people who choose to know and serve God, or choose not to. Anything other than that is not authentic."

"We don't have a choice because you either do what God tells you, or you go to hell," Bernard countered.

Over the course of a few months, Bernard persisted with his questions:

"Do you think something will take over humans someday?"

"How did we get all the races?"

"What's going to happen at the end of the world?"

"How do you know if there's a heaven and a hell?" Then he'd add, "No one can say they *know* they're goin' to heaven. They can only say, I *think* I'm goin' to heaven. Who would want to live forever anyway?" And he'd say, "Heaven would be boring just sitting around forever praising God. And there's no use praying. How could God hear all the people around the world praying to him all at once?"

Bernard knew some things about the Bible, and several times

brought up stories such as Jonah and the big fish, the Israelites cross-ing the sea, and Noah. And every once in a while, it seemed like Ber-nard may have even believed something he said he didn't. "Miracles don't happen nowadays like they did back then," he said once.

And that was how I got to know Bernard — a student and a homeless man sitting together at a table discussing life and theology. I admit he asked good questions. Hard ones.

Bernard also had things to say about those who believed in God. One time during a late-night conversation when I was volunteering at the Harvard Square Homeless Shelter, he said, "A lot of people who go to church don't care about me and you."

How do I respond to that? I wondered.

I felt like a defendant taking the witness stand, but Bernard had a point. "Well," I replied, "you may be right."

A couple of years before I went to Harvard, when I was a student at Anderson University School of Theology, each Friday evening sev-eral first-year undergraduate students piled in cars and pooled their cash, which they sometimes made by selling their plasma earlier in the week. They'd drive an hour to downtown Indianapolis, buy twenty Domino's pizzas and a sack of McDonald's double cheese-burgers, and hand them out to homeless people who awaited them each week, like people anticipating a birthday party. The students spent hours talking with them, and although I went with them only twice, I'll never forget a homeless man I met there named Chester.

I met Chester after he had moseyed by, long after the food was gone. He had a black eye that he said was a result of an assault by skin-heads a couple of nights before. Chester had a speech impediment and was at least a little intoxicated when we met. He eagerly told me about how God had provided him with food and some form of shelter each day of his twenty-five years on the streets.

What Chester did not have, though, were friends. He couldn't trust anybody on the streets, he said.

There was one person Chester did trust, however: my friend Caleb, a college freshman, who week after week had come to downtown Indianapolis with his friends to share in the lives of the city's homeless. Chester told me, with the same excitement I imagine he would have if he'd met the president of the United States, how Caleb had introduced his parents to him when Caleb and his family were walking through the city one night. Chester pointed to Caleb, who was standing nearby, then looked at me and said seven words that, although spoken with an impediment and missing some consonants, were said with perfect clarity: "I love him. I'd die for him." Weeks of faithful friendship — friendship that transcended cultural and socioeconomic barriers — had proven to Chester that Caleb was genuine and trustworthy.

Hearing Chester's testimony of Caleb's care helped me better see, up close and personal, how serving others can be an expression of God's love for both the givers *and* the receivers. It was moving to see students, much younger than me, bridging society's chasms and meeting needs of people on the streets.

Maybe Bernard formed his opinions because he didn't see Christians following Christ's teachings the way he thought they should. Maybe he was looking for people who were more righteous or for churches to better practice what they preached. I worry that I myself failed in providing such an example.

I didn't ever know much about Bernard's story. No one did. And although we saw each other quite often, we never became especially close.

Bernard said he didn't know how to turn on a computer, and I never saw him take a sip of alcohol. He bought scratch-off lottery tickets and admitted, "I'm kind of addicted to 'em," a common problem on the streets.

Bernard didn't use drugs, but once told me he had smoked a half-million cigarettes. Every cigarette I ever saw him smoke he rolled himself, using little white papers and shreds of the cheapest tobacco from a paper pouch. His fingernails, always stained a color between dark orange and brown, told the tale of his long-standing habit.

With all those cigarettes and experiences, though, came a lot of thinking and learning and the shaping of ideas that made him who he was and what he believed. With that, his story was a lot like the rest of ours.

And Bernard wasn't shy about speaking his mind.

"Good morning, Bernard," I said to him one morning.

"What's good about it?" he responded.

Bernard noticed how police enforced some laws and disregarded others, and was quick to point it out. "There's laws for the rich, and laws for the poor," he said. And after years of surveying Harvard Square, he'd say with a smile, "Harvard Square — the home of the haves and the have-nots, the sane and the insane."

He asked me once if I was going to be around the next winter, and I asked him the same question. "If I'm still alive," he said. As the summer progressed, Bernard's health problems seemed to escalate with neglect. "I'm ready for the grave," he told me at the end of July. Two days later, after much deliberation, Bernard went to the hospital. He was then transferred to a medical respite center for a long-term stay. Looking back now, I wish I had visited him when he was there. Bernard returned to the streets, but I heard later that he was eventually housed and was staying far away from his former life in Harvard Square.

Bernard always said that people who helped the homeless were really only interested in helping themselves. He would ask me pointedly, "You think there'd be a meal if someone wasn't making money off of it?" I doubted that the organizers of the meals were paid and assured him that the volunteers at the student-run shelter were just that—volunteers. I was one of them.

Even if Bernard was right, though, and those organizing and volunteering were paid or otherwise rewarded, would that be wrong? Would their service to the homeless be less admirable?

I had always thought that Bernard was just cynical, but I later thought that maybe what he had been saying had merit. Bernard's theory centered on the soul-searching inquiry into why we do what we do.

For those not paid for working in a charity, maybe the answer of why they volunteer *is* purely to help others or contribute positively to society. But maybe it's also to have a volunteer experience to put on a resume, or to learn what kind of career they might like to have. Maybe it's to find a mate who also enjoys helping others. Maybe it's to complete a sentence of community service mandated by a court, or to fulfill a class requirement to learn things that could never be learned inside the walls of a university.

Bernard wasn't alone in his opinions. Daryl, a homeless man I'd occasionally see, believed people looked down on the homeless unless they could get money from them through government grants or private donations that funded shelters or programs for addicts.

"Everyone who says they're doing good for people are only doing good for themselves," he argued. "The good are not as good," he'd say, "and the bad are even worse."

One day, Daryl had just found a bike and said he was planning to steal a part from another bike locked up next to where we were talking. I challenged Daryl about his plan to steal. He brushed it off, saying, "Being too good is bad and being too bad is bad," adding that it probably wouldn't even matter to the bike's owner, as if he were a blood relative.

What was it in Daryl's life that caused him to think that stealing was okay? I asked myself. *Street culture? His early life experiences? What?*

Even if it is true that some people — or all, as Bernard and Daryl would argue — do good for ulterior motives, is that necessarily entirely bad? Can good come out of narcissistic motives? Is it wrong for a student to volunteer at a nonprofit organization, offering her talents to help the homeless and further the mission of the charity, if she does it partly or solely to gain leadership experience for future employment opportunities? If she didn't do it, who else would? And what would their motives be?

A few years after Bernard shared his thoughts with me, my professor suggested I look at a book that wound up causing me to reflect on my conversations with Bernard and to further consider his insights. What I'd deemed as Bernard's cynicism a few years before had become words of wisdom. And as difficult as it was to admit, those insights helped me see the importance of checking my motivations when seeking to help others.

One of my homeless friends once said to me, "Everyone out here has a story." She mentioned how people tend to think that all homeless people are the same — losers and failures. But we knew that our friends on the streets were each unique — each with a name, a history, and a future. More often than not, though, it seemed their history was sad and their future grim. I can't help but believe that many people on the streets were deeply wounded — from hurts, addictions, shame, living situations, and relational disjointedness. For some, it seemed, hope had disappeared.

A teenager from the pit told me one day, with tears in her eyes, that the ten-year-old girl with cystic fibrosis she had half-raised had just died. Making matters even worse, someone to whom she had recently lent her phone had stolen it, and she had been out of touch with the family of the sick girl. And someone in our community once told me, long after he got off the streets, "I spent days going into Boston and looking at buildings and thinking, *I wonder how I can get on that roof and just end it all.* Then, all of a sudden, I'd think, *I can't do this. I have a little kid. I want to see my kid grow up.* I think any homeless person that says they don't think about that at some point is full of it. Every homeless person, I think, has their days. Then, all of a sudden, you pull yourself out of it. You have to. Otherwise you're not going to make it. My kid's the only reason I ever got through it. I kept saying, I'm going to watch my kid grow old."

But among the street's anguished alleys were rays of sunshine — people doing something to help. For years, the ministers and volunteers of the Outdoor Church have passed out food and shared words of encouragement to people on the streets of Cambridge every Sunday. Groups of Christians have come out to the streets regularly, such as members of the Streetlight Outreach, organized by a local church, and Starlight Ministries, organized by a local faith-based organization. They each came one night a week, sharing food and friendship with people on the streets. There were Spare Change Spencer's "angels," as he called them — young women who would walk by him every day on their way to and from work, caring enough to stop and chat. One Saturday, I met a young couple who, with their small child, passed out food once a month that they toted around in a plastic cooler. And there was Charlie, a faithful friend to the homeless, who generously bought people things just because he wanted to. Members of the Harvard Square Homeless Shelter's Street Team took food and clothes to people on the streets six nights a week, several weeks each semester. And Fig Newton Man, an older gentleman, sometimes came around in the early morning hours passing out Fig Newtons, and sometimes quarters, to the homeless. Jared maintained that he was a retired Harvard proctologist who wanted to make sure the homeless didn't have any trouble staying regular. I'm quite sure he was simply a gentle man who just wanted to be friendly with people living on the streets. Then there were students who'd come out to talk with homeless people or just chat with them while they were visiting the Square, including my friends Ruth and Melissa, both students at Wellesley College, who one weekend bought Chubby John a new Bible. Chubby John happily showed it to me, and one time I heard him say, "I read the Twenty-third Psalm out of my Bible. It really is easier to read. It's in everyday language."

These were all individuals who were concerned about the needs they'd seen in their community and did something to try to help. Maybe it was big; maybe it was small. But it was something, and that made a difference.

For many of us, no matter how much time we've spent with the homeless, we still find ourselves struggling with how best to help those we encounter on the streets, and with gaining the courage to do it. We're aware of the situations some people are in and might feel compelled to offer them something. We might feel we have something to share with them — spiritual, material, or social support. We're aware that Jesus offered to help people with their physical and spiritual needs. Yet we wonder, What should I do when I see a panhandler? What is the best way I can help a homeless person?

People have told me of the sadness they've felt when seeing homeless individuals, along with their confusion about how best to help them. Often all of that is complicated by the normal fears and awkwardness of a first encounter with a stranger.

An acquaintance of mine met me one day over the summer to ask for advice. Sitting on a park bench near CVS, she described a struggle she faced. As a Christian, she believed she needed to befriend and help the homeless. But she was unsure how to do it. "The best gift you can give is something they're not even asking for," I told her. "And that's a relationship."

A fellow member of the Harvard Square Homeless Shelter's Street Team once told me how she had wanted to say hi to Bernard while walking through the Square when she was not on her shift, but her anxieties kept her from doing so. It wasn't until she moved past that awkwardness by giving him money that she felt the door of communication unlock, opening an invitation to enter into conversation. Similarly, I have found at times that having something in my backpack, like a pair of new socks, for example, can serve as an ideal icebreaker to talk with a homeless person. It gives a tangible reason to stop and talk. It shows a person panhandling on the street that he or she is being acknowledged.

My Street Team colleague later told me, "I didn't like that I felt that way, because it felt like giving money was the easy way out. In other words, people always think they are doing good for homeless individuals when they give them money, and feel good about themselves when they do it. But I think it takes more courage just to talk to them, or at least look them in the eye and acknowledge their humanity."

Shortly after I began my summer on the streets, my friend Josh said to me, "What you are doing inspires me. Last night I had dinner with a homeless man. Knowing you and what you're doing makes me more aware of homeless people, and makes me have more compassion for them." Yet Josh still needed practical advice "to be kind and be smart," as he put it.

Helping people with both tangible and intangible needs is important. That's what my friends at Anderson University worked hard doing for the people on the streets of Indianapolis. Really understanding others' brokenness, hurts, and pain includes acknowledging our similarities — seeing people on the streets as equals, as people with rights, and as individuals with a desire to love and be loved.

Just as we look at receiving medical care or education in our society within the context of justice, maybe we should also look at relationships within the context of justice. Maybe people have a right to be in relationship with others, just as they have a right, because they are human, to have food or clothes. This relational justice is rooted in our own awareness that we'd not be where we are today without the support of others.

There's something inside each of us that needs other people. There's something inside each of us that longs to communicate with people who care, to feel a friend's embrace, maybe even to have the road dog friends Neal had spoken of.

When Neal gave me the cross that he paid four dollars for, his gift was like an invitation to friendship. Doris also gave me a cross that summer, and after the summer was over, another homeless person gave me a bigger cross — one she'd made out of sticks and twisted grapevines and had varnished so that it shined — that still, to this day, hangs above my bed. These crosses were not only symbols of personal faith and spiritual truths; they were objects that brought us closer to one another. They were symbols that could help us remember our need for restoration that only Christ could provide.

When we see a homeless person, we might be challenged with a moral conundrum, one that is often resolved by the giving of a coin or something else tangible. The problem I've continued to struggle with is that if I give someone something, I too often feel relieved of any further obligation to that person. It's easy for me to think, *I've done my good deed, and he can seek someone else for help in the future, should he need it.* But I know that he will need more help. I also know that if I look deep into my soul, I probably have not done all that I could have done to help him. Instead, the kind word or tangible good could be a launching point for further relating to each other.

Lately, though, I've considered the importance of relational authenticity — being open about the motivations behind a relationship. I've wondered how intentionality and being a genuine friend might be incongruous. I've wondered how often I've been guilty of being disingenuous, seeing a relationship for its utilitarian purpose or becoming friends with people for self-serving reasons. It's led me to evaluate the motivations behind the relationships that I have had, especially those I've initiated.

The more I think about the need to truly care for others, the more I realize how much I have failed. The more I look into my own heart, the more I see my selfishness, my hypocrisy, my excuses that I'm busy, my tendency to judge people as mentally ill or as helpless addicts whom I'm unable to change. Since moving away from Harvard, I've struggled with myself, asking, What am I doing to help others in need? How can I better interact with or assist those on the streets in the city in which I now live, as well as those in need throughout the world? When I honestly think about those questions, I see my shortcomings. I see how I view my time as a personal possession, rather than as a commodity to invest in others. I see my tendency to justify what little I may have done as being wholly sufficient. I see my tendency to withhold what I could give of myself. I see how I have fallen short.

Maybe looking at myself and seeing my deficiencies is the best place to begin changing. Maybe my time is not *my* time but something that belongs to God. Maybe such understandings are really central to implementing a theology of relational care.

Building relationships with people is better done within a conversation we have with ourselves that answers the question, How can I build relationships with others in a relationally authentic way? This helps ensure that our actions are sincere and not simply done out of what we may feel is an obligation or primarily for our own purposes. If we allow God to indwell us, perhaps our understanding of relationships, and the time it takes to develop relationships, can be transformed within us.

About halfway through the summer, I started reflecting on how the path to homelessness begins. For some, it began as children in dysfunctional families and neighborhoods. Some people I knew on the streets had a parent introduce them to substances that would haunt them like the black-hooded Grim Reaper, like a teenager I knew who told me his mother had introduced him to marijuana when he was seven years old. "You're old enough to know what this is," she had told him. I began seeing some people on the streets as victims — victims of the unfortunate actions of others, at an early age, over which they possibly had no control. For others, the path to homelessness was paved with decisions they had made themselves, perhaps influenced by people in their lives. Regardless of their circumstances, when people are addicted to substances, the addiction can control their actions, landing them on the streets and keeping them stuck there.

Mental illness also plays a role in the lives of many on the streets. It can affect people in a way that their illness ultimately controls their actions, while also complicating issues of substance abuse.

Some people have habits or are prone to profligacy, while others are victims of economic hardship and job loss. There was one man in the homeless community, though, who always made it clear that he blamed only himself for the situation he was in. "It's easier to blame somebody than take responsibility yourself," he'd say.

The needs in our world can be overwhelming. We know there are people who are hungry. We know that people are victims of abuse, terror, and war. We see them on TV. We read about them in magazines. But while we know people are hurting, we're not always sure how to alleviate those hurts. As we live, we want to be responsible — responsible to God, others, and ourselves. That may mean transforming a handout into something more than what a person asks for. It may mean engaging with the homeless and developing relationships, when possible, acknowledging that in many ways they are just like you and me. The difficulty, for most of us, is putting into action our awareness that people — in our own communities and all around the world — are in need of something we may be able to provide.

Lately, my ponderings have been complicated by wondering how to accurately discern need. Does everyone who asks me for something really need it? Could I possibly, through a helping act, be enabling someone to continue harming himself? Who might need my charity who isn't even asking for it?

Being responsible means being honest and wise about who has the greatest needs — ourselves or others — and then acting on that realization. It means being aware of the needs of others in the world and not forgetting about them, even though we've never met them and they're not sitting on our city's sidewalks directly asking us for something. It means being committed to discerning people's needs and being eager to fulfill them — even needs of those who live far away. It means doing our part to meet the social, emotional, and spiritual needs of people in our communities and our world, extending our care and concern to people — homeless or not homeless — who are hurting or lonely. For it is when we *know* others, and reach out to those we don't know, that we are able to extend greater love and care to them.

One rainy summer morning that, at fifty-nine degrees, felt more like October than July, several of us gathered inside the Red Doors Church. During the week, the church kept its doors unlocked while parents brought their children to the church's daycare center.

The Red Doors Church welcomed the homeless, and inside they drank coffee the sexton brewed each morning and used the restrooms, while others lingered and relaxed or charged their cell phones. Cell phones may not be what first comes to mind when you think about a homeless person, but they were an important means of communication within our community. Some people, like Chubby John, treasured their cell phones. Someone else in our community despised them and threw every one his sister gave to him into the Charles River — because she hassled him too much, he said.

On this particular day, I sat in the Red Doors Church for three hours with Bernard, Dane, and a young man from the pit who wore black clothes and metal spikes around his neck, watching the rain come down like it might not stop all summer. The four of us had a conversation about God and the Bible that was sort of like an impromptu church council — the Council of the Red Doors — that, I believe, started out with the subject of homosexuality.

"I'm pretty sure there's something in the Bible somewhere about not lying with your own gender," Dane said. "But there's nothing against being homeless in the Bible," he later noted.

"Nope," I said. "Foxes have holes and birds have nests, but Jesus said he didn't have any place to lay his head," I said, paraphrasing a Bible verse.

Bernard and I sat next to each other on the wooden bench just inside the doors. Perhaps it was the cold rain that caused his ponderings to surface like budding winter crocuses.

"I wonder about the first time a man shaved. Why did he want to shave?" Bernard asked me. "And how about the first time somebody smoked? How'd they start to think about doing that?" Then he turned to those he knew on the streets who spent the benefits they received from the government, because of their psychiatric diagnoses, on alcohol and drugs. "I don't understand why people get checks and then spend it on booze and drugs, and the government keeps giving it to them. The government should check up on them, and if they spend it on wrong things, then don't give it to them."

It seemed like a good idea. *The government is good about ensuring accountability with taxes and grants and contracts,* I thought. *Why not with the money they give out in benefits? I suppose it would be an auditing nightmare.*

Bernard continued, "Why don't they have an adopt-a-homeless-person program, like you can adopt a kid?" Without any prompting, he acknowledged the risk that some homeless people might "clean out the house at night."

"If there was a stray dog outside, somebody would take it in," he said. "But they don't do anything about the homeless people. People are too quick to judge. They see one drunk and they think they're all that way."

It seemed Bernard was perhaps again focusing his comments and his "adopt-a-homeless person" idea at Christians. "If somebody's a real Christian," he had once told me, "they should take homeless people in."

Echoing those views again that morning at the Red Doors Church, he said, "Christians are the least likely to help. They preach it, but don't live it."

"It seems fears and society prevent people from taking strangers into their homes," I said, trying to be delicate.

"They could get to know them," he countered.

"I agree," I said.

Maybe feeling a bit defensive, I posed an alternative argument. "Whose responsibility is it to take care of someone?" I asked. "Is it my responsibility to take care of me? Your responsibility to take care of you?" I paused, thought, and responded to what had just come out of my mouth. "Or maybe we should just try to take more care of each other."

eight

911

I see Neal!" Amy shouted to Chubby John and me as we glanced across thousands of people spread across the massive lawn in front of the outdoor stage. Looking for Neal in the masses was like trying to find a friend at a Six Flags amusement park; you know he's there, but finding him is nearly impossible. We did have an advantage, though: Neal's towering height and bright red ball cap. And that was enough reason to give us hope that we might eventually find him.

Neal had been talking about seeing the Temptations for two weeks, singing his favorite songs of theirs and planning how he was going to stake out a seat at the outdoor venue in Boston. He knew that if he wanted a good seat — and nobody wanted to have a good seat more than Neal — he'd have to get there early for the free concert.

Somehow, among the thousands of dreamy-eyed, Motown-fever-struck fans, Chubby John, Amy, Neal, and I — although we had come separately to the performance — all made our way to each other. It was a small marvel.

Amy said Neal was sitting in the "active section," where people danced and enjoyed the music as if they were reliving life in the mid-1960s, although many there weren't even alive then. From the middle of the crowd, Chubby John, Amy, and I navigated a path, squeezing our way between countless lawn chairs, blankets, and coolers, working our way through the obstacle course toward Neal and the stage, as if we were on a great trekking expedition.

Neal and Amy danced as the Temptations sang "How Sweet It Is (To Be Loved by You)," while the rest of us enjoyed the contagious beat. A little while later, a man from a group of people sitting next to us asked Amy to dance. For Amy, the dance was mere amusement and harmless fun. But as Neal watched Amy with her new partner, he rubbed his face and put his head down. I knew that he treasured Amy in a way he probably hadn't treasured anyone in a long time.

A few minutes later, Amy left us to resume the picnic she had been having with her other friends. It didn't seem like Neal realized she was even leaving, though, meditating as if he'd been stunned by bad news.

After the concert, Chubby John, Neal, and I meandered back to the subway station. "That guy who danced with Amy — he used the f-word every other word," Neal said, still agitated, adding some choice words about how the man was a drug addict and had no business dancing with Amy.

The subway was packed with fellow concertgoers herding through the gates into the subway like shoppers on Black Friday. Chubby John and I touched our subway passes to the gate sensors and entered, but Neal apparently didn't have a subway pass and the alarm sounded after he followed someone through the gate. A subway guard, stationed in front of the gates, ordered Neal to go back, while Chubby John and I waited on the other side.

In no time, though, Neal appeared among the masses, walking through the gate, standing straight and carrying his duffle bag like a liberated man exiting a jail. Amy followed him through the gate, smiling, having paid for his entry with her pass. There it was again — another small marvel — Amy reuniting with us at just the right time.

On the subway ride back to Harvard Square, Neal said in a fatherly sort of way, "I've got something to talk to you about, Amy. Don't ever dance with a drunk junkie again. And he had another girl — why did he need two?"

Amy seemed to understand. "Okay, I'm sorry," she responded. "I need to learn to say no. Good tip. You're a much better dancer anyway. No comparison."

Amy, of course, wouldn't have wanted to hurt anyone. Like Doris once told me, "She's like the light who comes around and brightens our day." On the streets, though — just like anywhere — misunderstandings, disagreements, and conflicts could involve just about everyone — including Amy, including me. Fortunately, quarrels over the summer often ended congenially. No doubt, there were a lot of them.

Only just that afternoon, in fact, on the day of the Temptations concert, Chubby John had walked a few feet away from his stemming spot next to CVS to come over and say something to me. Before he could reclaim his spot, though, a man I didn't know in a wheelchair wheeled up next to CVS and immediately started saying, "Spare change?" to passersby. Chubby John, not appreciating his spot being taken from under him, told him that he should leave. "You're not even homeless!" John said to the man. "He does this a lot," John said to me, as if the man couldn't hear him. "He lives with his sister."

When resolution seemed unthinkable, Dane happened upon the scene, like a peacemaking superhero. I don't remember what Dane said or how he did it, but from the mouth of one who said things such as "love is a gift; it comes to you when you're worthy" and "the essence of life is joy" came enough wisdom to compel Chubby John and the man in the wheelchair to shake hands and speak like friends. It was quite remarkable, really.

Although Dane was a peacemaker, he could get agitated like anybody else. One time, Dane was upset about not getting any free pizza from the leftovers the Upper Crust Pizzeria set out when they closed. Some nights there were several boxes, most of which were full. Other nights, there were few or none. Each white cardboard pizza box was always like a wrapped present whose contents were a mystery; we never knew exactly what we'd find inside.

This particular night, Dane walked by the pizzeria too late, long after the pizzas were gone. I think Dane thought that others in the community had taken more than they should have, and that's why there wasn't any pizza left that night. Chubby John told him that no one had taken too much and that pizza had been available for several people. The argument resembled what I'd guess a live performance of the *Jerry Springer Show* — "The Pizza Episode" — would be like. But remarkably, a few minutes after Dane steamed off, he returned, shook Chubby John's hand, and apologized. Just like Neal always said, Harvard Square was better than television.

But that was nothing compared with one particular night when Chubby John said he spotted a PVC pipe hidden down the back of Please Leave Larry's pants. Thankfully, Please Leave Larry didn't brandish it, and no fight broke out. Only one pizza was available that night, and Please Leave Larry and his friends took it, leaving the rest of us without. Later, on Neal's Island, Please Leave Larry walked by and told Chubby John, "There's leftover pizza in the pit." But Chubby John thought it was just a trick to lure him into trouble.

"How could there be pizza left when there was only one box tonight?" Chubby John asked us.

Please Leave Larry had already tried to fight Chet that morning, according to word on the street. I'd heard that Please Leave Larry wanted to set up Chet in front of the police, just to get Chet in trouble. When Chubby John heard about Please Leave Larry's plans, he foiled them by warning Chet to stay away.

The next day, Chubby John said Please Leave Larry had spoken with him, assuring Chubby John that he'd had no intention of fighting him. The pipe the night before had been for him to use against someone else.

Someone told me later, "There's one reason Please Leave Larry is called Please Leave."

Near the end of the summer, the Upper Crust Pizzeria decided to end its practice of leaving its pizza leftovers outside, because of messes that had been left in the Square. Fortunately, though, the managers of the pizzeria were happy to continue giving out nightly leftovers to designees who'd make sure that the pizzas and their boxes would not litter the Square. Spare Change Spencer, Hank, and I served as those designees, going into the pizzeria at night to collect the pizzas and then distributing them on the streets. We explained to people the importance of keeping the Square clean, and the managers were more than happy about the arrangement; sometimes they even provided us with two-liter bottles of soda.

"Everybody got fed," Dane happily said one night. "We're gonna miss you out here," he told me. "You really fit in. You're like a cog in the wheel. At first you were so naive out there with the cup in the traffic. Now you have street instincts," he said. "You'll really appreciate inside life more now, having been out here."

A few days earlier, Dane had praised me for spending the summer with them on the streets. "At first he'd come out here and give out food and listen and encourage us to talk," Dane announced to me, and whoever may have been listening, about my work with the Shelter's Street Team. "And then he came out and said he was going to live with us. And I thought, *Yeah, that will last a couple of days.* But he had Neal mentor him, and now you're looking at a well-seasoned bum."

"Well, I'm still working on that," I said with a smile.

I wish I could say that I did a great deal more for the homeless than distribute leftover pizzas for a few nights, but I can't. And one of the regrets I have from that summer is that I didn't do more with my head and my hands than listen and jot down notes.

Chubby John said one time that there were a couple of guys he knew who asked what I was doing for the homeless. They weren't the only ones. Doris also had poignant things to say to me. However, despite what Doris said, I like to think that down deep, she appreciated our relationship. She had once given me a metal cross on a string necklace, which I kept in my pocket next to the one Neal had given me.

Doris is the one who had come up with a nickname for me, Divinity John, that had stuck among some in our community. She was intelligent and a critical thinker; she also liked using big words around me and occasionally corrected my grammar.

"You know what the difference is between you and me and all the rest of us out here?" she asked me. She told me the answer more than once to make sure I didn't forget. "Nobody's out here telling me I'm doing a good job for being homeless."

Doris was exactly right. I had done nothing that deserved commendation or admiration from anyone. I was merely sleeping outside, going to class, and spending time in the library. I hadn't done anything special. I was not homeless; she was.

Doris and the rest of my homeless friends were living in the world of homelessness all the time, some without any hope of ever permanently leaving the streets. They were on the streets whether they liked it or not. And down deep, nobody liked it. Although Neal was able to return to his mother's home anytime, and did so periodically, he yearned for the chance to room with James. Chubby John was on his way off the streets by the end of the summer and into an apartment that he'd acquire through a housing assistance program. Dane soon wound up in the hospital from complications to his foot after having his toe removed the previous year, and he soon had a room of his own in a rooming house. And not long after the summer was over, Spare Change Spencer found a place to live in another state.

My talks with Doris were some of the most uncomfortable of the summer. When she was drunk, I knew she was going to say things I didn't want to hear.

While Doris, like others, wanted to know how I was helping the homeless, one of the several things she criticized me about was perpetuating a stereotype of the homeless; by seeming to live as a homeless person, I was adding to the stigma of the homeless, rather than actively disrupting it. Another criticism I heard from others was for drawing attention to myself when I could have shifted that attention to greater awareness of those who were really in need. They were right.

In my eagerness to experience and share about what it is like to be homeless, I'd planned to do more than necessary to get a look inside the world of homelessness. I probably didn't really need to blend in with the homeless community to do that. Looking back, I see that thinking that I could become an actual insider was inaccurate. In reality, I'll probably never have a true experience of homelessness.

Spending time on the streets with the homeless that summer provided extended time with the community I had become acquainted with during my first year at Harvard. I had hopes of learning more about homelessness in a way I never had before, and of writing about my experience and sharing stories about homelessness with people who were, like I once was, unfamiliar with life on the streets. I wanted to help non-homeless people understand a culture and people that might be unknown or even scary to them. To accomplish this, I had hoped to better understand what the homeless *did*. My summer on the streets, however, helped me better understand who the homeless *are*.

I hoped that my story of bridging the gap between the homeless and non-homeless would, ultimately, help homeless people. Hopefully, the self-serving nature of my time on the streets can be redeemed by what the experience has taught me, and what others might learn from it as well. By opening a window into the lives of those who dwell on the streets, maybe — just maybe — people will have a little more understanding of those who are homeless.

While I might not have directly helped the homeless a great deal that summer, I hope that I somehow helped them indirectly. Yes, I could have volunteered at an organization that summer, like I'd volunteered on the Shelter's Street Team during the school year, but I wouldn't have had quite the same experience. I wouldn't have seen the same things I did by spending time on the streets, and I may not have met most of the people who became my friends that summer. If people had looked at my Harvard colleague who was co-managing a nearby summer shelter, they wouldn't have asked twice about how she was helping the homeless. But I wasn't managing shelters or preparing meals for the homeless that summer. There are lots of things that I didn't do, and many things I probably could have done. For sure, though, what little good I might have done was far outweighed by the good my homeless friends did for me.

Being criticized on the streets isn't a private thing that stays between two people. One homeless person had coined the term "homeless gossip" to describe the way word traveled on the streets and once told me, "There are no secrets among the homeless."

Dane encouraged me. "What other people think of you doesn't matter to you. They could think the same thing about that lamp pole." Maybe it was Dane's feelings about his own self-esteem that helped him feel sympathy toward me. Spare Change Spencer also said, "People out here are supposed to be your friends. If somebody thinks you're a bad person, and you're not, who cares? Eventually they'll find out," he said. "There's a difference between understandin' what people believe and carin' about it. Don't let negativity bring you down."

Despite some of the things Doris had said to me — and I commend her for saying them to my face, rather than behind my back — by the end of the summer, she was commenting that we were all a family. One evening, during a meal at the Red Doors Church, she looked at all of us and announced, "I look forward to coming to this meal even if I'm not hungry, just so I can see you all and talk about my problems. You know about my problems; you know where I sleep. My daughters don't even know as much about me as you do," she told us.

"We are a family," Chubby John said, a bit sarcastically, as he returned to the table. "You're my brother ... or maybe my sister," he kidded with one of the men sitting with us.

Five days later, a couple of people from Doris's street family found her late one evening sitting on the sidewalk in front of the Red Doors Church, needing to talk. I was checking my email at a building on campus, but I caught up with them and sat down on the sidewalk next to Doris.

"We've helped her as much as we could," one of our friends said to me. "But you're the best one out here to help her."

Under the open sky, Doris was surveying all of the difficulties of her life, none of which I had ever experienced. She worried about somewhere she had to go the next day and all that had transpired in her adult life up to that point. As she spoke, I listened, offering words of encouragement and counsel when I felt they were necessary. Doris didn't want me to leave her, so after she got tired of sitting on the sidewalk, we went to the cranny where she slept each night, hidden away where she could feel somewhat safe. She settled into her sleeping bag and I read to her from her Bible, by candlelight, until she fell asleep.

Relationships within the homeless community certainly weren't like those of a traditional family, but many people did have connections — good or bad — with others on the streets. A couple of days after the Temptations concert, Neal said to me, "You know, I have three friends." Then, counting off the numbers on his fingers, he said, "Jared." Pointing to his second and third fingers, he said, "John — that's you. And Amy." Then he shrugged in disappointment. "Make friends, then they leave," he said, referring to Amy's impending departure to Europe. To Neal, Amy's three-week vacation seemed like something permanent.

The day came for us all to say goodbye to Amy. For me, saying goodbye was, in fact, like saying goodbye for good. I had tentatively planned to leave the streets about the time she'd be returning from her trip, and because I wasn't sure if I was going to stay in the Boston area after the summer, we didn't know if we'd see each other again. Ultimately, I decided to add a couple more weeks to my time among the homeless, which allowed me to continue the friendships I had developed and provided more opportunities for experiences that I could hopefully share with others. I saw Amy in the Common after the Outdoor Church was over and she handed me a little gray envelope with "Divinity John" written on the front of it. Amy passed out notes in little envelopes to others as well, along with pictures she'd taken.

She talked to Neal and Chubby John for a long time on Neal's Island before leaving.

"Bye, honey," Neal said, after hugging her goodbye. "Just when you get to know somebody ..." he trailed off.

Chubby John said to me, "He thinks he'll be dead before she comes back."

"Did he tell her that?" I asked.

"No," Chubby John said. "He's gettin' worse every day; can't ya tell? He sleeps more every day."

Just a few days before, Neal had asked James and me to promise him that if we found him dead someday, we'd take his identification so no one would know he died, namely his mother. He worried that his death would cause his mother to have a stroke. However, he said that if she died before he did, he'd be angry. James and I dodged Neal's request by insisting that the police would know him with or without an ID.

Amy's leaving and giving us those notes made me feel sad — sentimental — as I remembered the good times we'd all had together.

I had seen the homeless community embrace her and watched her become friends with them. Her leaving — in Neal's book — was the end of an era. I felt the same way.

A few hours after saying goodbye, however, Neal seemed to have bounced back. "I'm a drunk," he told me, "but you gotta admit, people like me. You know why? Cause I'm happy-go-lucky. I'm not mean or abusive." But then reality hit again and he missed Amy.

To make matters worse, his hope of rooming with James was dissipating into a distant dream that faded more each day. Neal was realizing that what he wanted was simply not going to happen. In a way, it was a snapshot of other aspects in his life, his hopes turning into disappointments.

About a week later, while waiting for James, Neal sat painting an old clay flowerpot he'd found in some bushes somewhere. He always had a way with plants. One day, not too long before, Neal had shown me a little Norway maple seedling that he had replanted from a plastic cup into a bamboo pot. He hid it in the bushes in the cemetery and said he wanted to make a bonsai out of it. He was waiting for James that day too. I suggested that we go to Harvard's Museum of Natural History, but he hoped James would stop by and said that storing his cart while we went inside the museum would be a problem anyway.

The clay pot Neal was painting was much bigger than any other pot he had. "It's very old. It's an antique, like three hundred years old," Neal said, happily showing me his new find. "I want to take it to my mother's, or my place, if James ever gets that room," he said. But with each stroke of his paintbrush, his hopes of that actually happening withered.

"My biggest pet peeve, John, is when somebody says they're going to do something and they don't. A man's word is his honor."

I sat and watched him paint as frustration clouded over him. "I may be a drunk, but I'm a good person," he continued.

I asked him about the work the room needed before he and James could move in. Neal responded cynically, "Yeah, that was like three weeks ago. It's just a room. It's not even a big apartment. You know how long it would take me to paint it? One day. C'mon."

Neal soon got word that he would see the room with James sometime that week. Chubby John was even talking about how Neal would move away and find new friends elsewhere, and we'd never see him again. But James didn't come. And Neal stayed tending to his bonsai and clay pot.

Neal's spirit was diminishing. He wasn't going to move indoors; he couldn't look forward to being housed with a friend. Amy had left; he couldn't look forward to her visits. His health was deteriorating; he couldn't look forward to waking up feeling well.

Later that week, Chubby John texted me. Neal had been taken to the hospital. When I saw Chubby John later that evening, he explained the whole ordeal in detail. He said that Neal had become sicker, that Hank called 911, and that he had heard Neal rattle off his medical conditions to the paramedics, all of which surprised Chubby John.

Chubby John looked at me and said, "It really is true. He really is dying."

In the words of NEAL

I'll be dead soon. I don't have a doctor; I have a team of doctors. I have hepatitis C and B, and my liver has been cirrhotic since about the late nineties. That's because of the vodka. Before, I was drinking half Gatorade, half vodka, in those Gatorade containers. For fifteen years I drank like that, every day. If I had just stuck with the beer, I probably wouldn't have cirrhosis. I bled into my stomach a couple years ago. I was in a coma for three and a half days. The doctor told my mother I probably wouldn't make it. I pretty much died and I came back. And George was there in the room, and my mother, and my friend Kirby.

And I have AIDS. My last T-helper cell count was like 120. It's supposed to be between 750 and 1,200. And when you lose them, your immune system goes down. I think I got it from shooting needles and sharing them in the late '80s. But I never really was a junkie. I just did it a few times. But it only takes once. Someone had the virus. When you're HIV positive for twenty-four years like me, you just get used to it after a while. After a while you start feeling like, I'm probably never going to die of it. So I just drink my beer and play on my guitar.

I'd like to be healthier. I don't want to die, but I know I'm going to.

It's a scary thing to die. What makes the thought of death tolerable is knowing that everyone has to go with you. Imagine if you were the only one that had to die; it would be awful. I know I have to do it someday, so what's the difference between now or when I'm eighty years old? You have to face it someday.

Basically, I'm just working on my plan out before I leave this world. I need to start painting because I know I can paint. I want to leave something behind.

I know if I got sober, I'd do more things. But getting sober is becoming a new creature. I don't know what it's like to live sober. I'd be like afraid of that. It's a big fear for a guy who's been drinking as long as I have. To be sober and not drink anymore? That's preposterous! I've been sober for like three months — that's my record. But I was in a hospital. That's not the same as being out here in the world. When you live out here and are sober, *that's* being sober. When you're in a hospital program, with a bunch of other guys, and you're all getting doped together, it's easier.

I'd like to have a number-one hit song on the radio. I don't care who performs it. If I do it, that's fine; if someone else does it, that's fine. And also, I'd like to finish my book. It's a bunch of short stories called *Jessie Street*. It's about things that happened in my life, like the first chapter — "The Park" — refers to Golden Gate Park, where I lived for eleven years. I just have a bunch of ideas for chapters, but I don't have the patience to be a writer. Somebody said it the best: "Writers write." If you don't write, you're not a writer. But I know I can write. The ideas and short stories are all in my mother's cellar. My crazy childhood would probably be in the book. I think if I could explain my childhood, you'd know why I'm the way I am now. It's all connected.

The reason I titled the book *Jessie Street* is because one time I was walking down the street in San Francisco. I had no money. I was dirty. I was hungry. I was so depressed I wanted to kill myself. And I saw this street sign, and it was all crooked and bent. It said "Jessie Street." I looked down the street and it was just a dead end — all big, old brick factory buildings, with boards over the windows. It was the most depressing street I ever saw. It had an old, beat-up sidewalk. There wasn't one bit of wind. It was perfectly still. And all of a sudden, this warm breeze came out of nowhere and came right into my face, and I instantly became happy. And I knew in that wind was the presence of God. I'll never ever forget that day.

I think God comes to me when I'm down and out, at the bottom of the heap, when I'm really bad off, when I'm so bad off I need a crutch or something, when I'm just totally miserable, which doesn't happen that often. I can get a little bit depressed here and there. They said I was bipolar years ago. But I don't see it. Well, maybe it's coming back. I don't know.

When I was younger, I used to care what people thought of me. But now I don't care. I know and God knows. I couldn't care less what others think. You could come up to me and say, "You know what, Neal? You're a scumbag jerk." And I'd go, "Uh-huh." It doesn't even faze me. I used to get angry at that. Now you could say anything you want insulting to me, and I just think, *I know who I am. God knows who I am. I know what I am. And God knows what*

I am. It doesn't matter what anybody else thinks I am. I've come to that conclusion. It's like solving an algorithm.

Just be who you are. That's what I've learned in fifty-four years.

I have so many regrets. I didn't write my book. I didn't get a rock band together. Didn't have children. There's a million of them. I never felt like I was good enough, even though I know I am good enough. Something in my head tells me I'm not good enough. And I can't explain it. It's just like a self-defeating attitude.

When something unjust happens to me, I get mad. I go, "You know what, God? You screwed me over again." I yell at God. And then something good happens to me, and I have to apologize to God. That's how I work. It's kind of like a little roller coaster. I don't blame him for doing something to me. I get mad because he didn't help me when I was trying to be a good person.

Jesus takes care of me, like the lilies of the field. I don't keep the constant contact, the constant prayer. A lot of times I'm very forgetful. I just keep working more; I just keep trying better.

If I admit that I'm nothing, only then can I become something.

In the words of

DANE

*T*he first time I heard Smokey Robinson singing "The Tears of a Clown," I so identified with that song. All my life I have felt unworthy of others. I have always felt that I had to please people to enjoy their company. Just Dane off the rack wasn't ever good enough. I had to be something more. A little funnier, a little louder, a little more animated. So my life has kind of been a play where I pretend that everything is alright and that nothing bothers me. Dane is like the sad, lonely clown whose tears are hidden by the painted-on smile. I still fight to this day with my self-worth. My self-esteem is always an issue in relationships. I get jealous, and I get possessive because I don't feel like I'm worthy to keep someone special in my life.

For a number of years, I was stealing and sneaking around, doing despicable things. People would go to work and save for things, and I would come and break in and steal them and smoke them up in an hour. I remember there was a girl who had all these antiques in her apartment, and I had a buyer for china and porcelain. I broke into that girl's apartment and I stole all of her objects. The next day she moved out.

I used to say to people that I don't do violent crimes. I have never confronted a person in the commission of a crime. I never brandished a weapon. And this guy said to me, "You violated that woman's personal space. Violate and violence are very close. You did violence to that woman emotionally and psychologically."

And maybe *man* didn't get to take note because I didn't get arrested, but *God* knows. For me it just piled another stone on my chest, so to speak. Truly, I am worthless.

But I'm just a person. We learn through trial and error, and, God, you put us here without a handbook, and I don't know how to act. I learned something from my mother and something from my father, and something from somebody else. I was never sure if you were really there, God, and right and wrong just seemed all relative. I'm just a human, and you made me this way — to falter and to fail. But don't I always get back up? Don't I keep trying?

That's how I talk to God.

I was married for fourteen years. The relationship was deteriorating. The fires had died out. Even the smoldering coals were no longer hot. The only friends I had were other cab drivers. I used to visit their bands. And I started getting introduced to cocaine in the men's room. My nostrils would flare, and suddenly I wasn't lonely, and my life wasn't empty, and I wasn't thinking about her and the kids. I thought, *I can do this on my own. I can live without them.* That's the thing that coke did for me. And so I started getting deep into it, and pretty soon the complaints stacked up, and they pulled my license, and I couldn't drive cab anymore. So now

I'm on the street. And I'm doing more and more coke, and I start stealing for it.

I was like a one-man crime wave out there. I got introduced to cooking it and smoking it, and that was the beginning of the end. To this day, even the smell of those fumes make me shudder. I see the gates of hell right before my eyes.

I regret, in retrospect, not having been there for my children growing up. I had to leave when my son was three and my daughter was eight. And I used to come and visit every weekend, but then one day my wife was on the phone and she said, "You know what our daughter said to me today after you left? She said, 'Mommy, sometimes when I have friends over and Daddy comes, he embarrasses me because he doesn't look right. He looks sick, or dirty.'" It was like a dagger in my heart that my princess could see the ravages of the road. And so I started coming around less and less.

One time my daughter was going to dance in the school play, and she said, "Daddy, Friday night, seven o'clock, at the school."

"Seven o'clock — I'll be there, Princess. I'll be there."

Friday night, about two thirty, I was sitting in the basement of a building on a milk crate with a candle and rats running around. I was smoking cocaine, and suddenly I remembered, *Friday at seven.*

And my son — his teachers would call my wife and say, "Could your son's father visit the class and speak to the children? Your son speaks of his father all the time. 'My father plays the guitar. My father drives a cab.'" The teacher said, "His father sounds like someone I think the kids could learn something from." It happened twice. I said I would be there, and I never showed up.

All those years when I used to dream about my kids, I always dreamt of them as three and eight. My memory of them froze in time, even though they had grown up. In my dreams, they were still the same age as when I left.

Today my children are in my life, thirty years later.

I was on cocaine for about twenty-eight years. I felt irredeemable. I was powerless. If a man has no hope, he has no future.

If you're going to align yourself with objects and materials and make them your gods — your little sub-gods — then God Almighty will not entertain any of that. I came to that point one night smoking cocaine. I was in a bathroom, and I was scared to death. I heard something outside the door, and I had this big rock of cocaine in my hand. I was sitting on the toilet using it like a chair. And I was saying, "God, help me, please!" My heart was pounding. I had a necklace of Jesus' head, and I was holding it in my hand. And all of a sudden, I heard like my own thoughts, *If you want my help, you must first begin by helping yourself. For I will not do for a man what he can do for himself. Now open your hand and drop that little god of yours into the toilet and flush it.* All of a sudden, I was like, "God, there's a little static on the line. Can I call you back?" And I hung up the phone on God. I smoked all of that stuff, and then the next day I was in jail.

Aurobindo, the spiritual master from India who I follow, had evening talks with the children after supper every night at the ashram. A young boy asked Aurobindo, "Oh, sir, if God is truly all loving and kind, as you often tell us, why is it then that men yet remain in bondage to pain and suffering?" And the old man smiled and said, "My child, men remain in bondage to pain and suffering only because men are in love with their chains." He said that it's not God's doing that you remain in pain and suffering. It's your own doing, because you are in love with that which confines you. You are in a prison of your own making, in a self-imposed exile from the mainstream of this creation, and you have the key to release yourself right in your pocket, and you won't use it.

I would go to Alcoholics Anonymous and Narcotics Anonymous meetings when I was in jail, and I'd say that this was the place where I come to get free. Out there on the street, I carry my cell around on my back. I have the only key and I won't let myself out. So God Almighty, who loves me dearly still to this day, sends his emissaries — the boys in blue — to break me out of my cell and take me to a place like this where I can get back to Dane. I have freedom in prison because I can't use drugs.

When I was in prison, there was an Episcopalian priest. He had a deal with Dunkin' Donuts, and he used to bring in about ten-dozen doughnuts. And he would come into the cellblock with five hundred cells, five tiers high. And he would yell, "Church and doughnuts at one o'clock!" And the officer would say to him, "Reverend, don't you know those guys only go to church for the doughnuts?" And he said, "Sir, God doesn't care why they come, because he knows they'll leave with a lot more than a doughnut."

When I was in jail, the only guitar was in the chapel. I started helping the pastor with playing music for the services. I had an ulterior motive originally. I was just trying to get near the guitar. I got in there and I got more than I came in for — a lot more. I started learning certain church songs and doing solos on the guitar. And then I thought, *I write songs; I could write a song appropriate to the church*. And so I set about attempting to do that. And that's how I began coming up with the Christian songs that I've written. I wrote all those songs in prison. I'm amazed at how much of Christianity I absorbed just playing guitar in the chapel.

There's an old saying in the program that says, "First the man takes the drug, then the drug takes the man." And that's what happens. You become a cocaine-using machine.

In 2008, I lost my big toe to an infection. I was wearing a pair of shoes a half-size too small, in the winter, and I was sitting out in seventeen-degree temperature panhandling for four-five-six hours, trying to get cocaine money. I used to get like seventy-five to a hundred bucks a day in my spot. And then I'd get on my bike and go buy the cocaine and smoke cocaine all night. And the next morning, I'd start over.

The toe became abraded by the tight shoe, and the abrasion became infected, and I wasn't maintaining it. When my sock started sticking to it, I just didn't take my sock off. I am diabetic, and I wasn't taking insulin. It got into the marrow. And I remember when the doctor was looking at the X-ray, he said, "Well, sir, this toe is mine."

I said, "Doc, you could use a refresher course in Bedside 101, dude."

And he said, "Do you want me to sugarcoat it? It's your toe! Where've you been, on vacation? It didn't happen overnight."

And he had me. What was I going to say, "Smoking cocaine"?

And over those six weeks that I laid in the hospital, I had an epiphany. I was looking at a piece of Dane missing. A piece of me that I gave to cocaine. And I asked myself, *How much more of me can I afford? A foot? A leg?*

I had to make a decision. And I decided I wasn't giving any more of me to cocaine. I thanked God for all the pain and the suffering that I endured to get to that epiphany. I was thinking of Popeye, one of my favorite philosophers: "That's all I can stands; I can't stands no more."

However, the next year, after I was clean, I got a retroactive check, and I did buy some cocaine. I opted to try one more time — to do it differently. I did it again. I was in stark terror the whole time. And I thought, *Wow, God is not going to allow this*. There was so much shame of knowing I shouldn't be doing this. God showed me there's nothing new in there; it's the same ol' agony. He showed me quickly, and it didn't cost me that much.

I believe that the essence of life is joy. However, there is a gap between what I believe and what I live day to day, moment to moment. I'm not always able to tap into that joy because I create the gap through my actions and inactions. And so I'm still learning that I am the creator of my own pain, my own sorrow. And there's no one else to blame.

Thank God that I feel bad about harm and hurt that I did to others. I thank God that I'm not so cold and callous that I cannot feel regret.

After having that epiphany — that enough was enough — and after having the obsession to use removed, I decided that under the throes of various and sundry addictions, I have been a constant, perpetual taker. All my life, the world has been my horn of plenty, and I just eat the fruit. It's like everybody had their own full glass and I just had a straw and I went around and dipped it in everyone else's glass. That's the way I was living — just taking. And I decided that God has sustained me thus far and has seen me through to the other side of that dark tunnel. And I prevail. Still I stand. And if God deems that I have any longevity whatsoever left on this earth, I choose now to spend it trying my best to give back some of what I have taken. To the best of my ability, present me with the work, and I will comply. That's the deal that I have struck with God.

There's more in me that I want to utilize. I still feel like I can do more. I want to reach more people. Now that I'm back on my own two legs, and in my own right mind, I wish to share with others my experience, my ill-gotten wisdom. I've suffered long and hard. I could save someone else the cost. I don't want to just go to my grave silently. I want to impart something into those who may be susceptible to the same forces that assailed me in life and caused me to veer off of the path.

I'm going out kicking and screaming, jumping and running. I hit the floor every morning, filled with vital exuberance on these nine toes and with this one good eye, and I don't care how close to seventy I am — and it's only four years away — I feel like I've got another twenty good years in me. And I'm going to spend them giving something back.

Nine

HOSPITALS AND HOTDOGS

In the intensive care unit, Neal was alert and talking, but attached to the kinds of medical devices and tubes that make a person look like he's dying. Although the rules technically allowed only two visitors at a time, Chubby John, another homeless friend, and I entered without any problem. We stood around his bedside and he told us how he was feeling. The next time I saw him, he'd been transferred to a different hospital.

"Hey, Neal," I said quietly as I entered his room at the other hospital.

"Who's that?" he asked groggily. Looking up and recognizing me, he said, "Hi, John," as if he wasn't surprised to see me or was bored. "I'm weak. I'm lethargic," he said.

I sat down on a padded plastic hospital chair at the foot of his bed. "Are there a lot of nice nurses here?" I asked, trying to lighten the mood.

"Beautiful," he replied.

I knew Neal was alright.

Neal drifted back to sleep. I suppose that when he had said, "As long as I can lay down, I'm happy. I'm happiest when I'm horizontal," he probably wasn't thinking about a hospital bed. And when he'd said, "I love being a bum. There's no one nagging me. I have complete freedom," he may not have been thinking about that lifestyle ending because of ill health.

Not long before, Neal had been wearing his red ball cap, laughing, puffing heavily on his homemade cigarettes, and blowing out big clouds of smoke. Not long before, he had been snapping his fingers and leaning against a tree, singing the words of a Journey song: "When the lights go down in the city ... So, you think you're lonely, well, my friend, I'm lonely too." He had sung it as though he were singing about his own loneliness. Then he stopped and said to me, "It's a love song, written about a city." Not long before, Neal had been making comments such as, "I'm so old-fashioned I love it when a woman curtsies. You know, lifts up her dress a little bit. That's how old-fashioned I am." Not long before, on Neal's Island, he had happily reported, "Not one time has the police come on this island. Except one time. A woman called the police when seeing me lying down under the tree. She could have gotten me in trouble," he had said, still agitated about it. "If I'm dead, I'm dead," he resolved. "If I'm not dead, I'm not dead. Don't call the police!"

These days, Neal had been talking more about death. In the hospital, though, Neal had other things on his mind. Before I left, he told me he was worried whether his money was still in his billfold. Remembering from when my grandmother was in the hospital how a patient's belongings are usually stored in a plastic bag in the room, I looked in a cupboard for Neal's street clothes, where I found them just as I'd expected.

I reached for his jeans and pulled from the pocket his large leather billfold. I stood beside his bed, opened it up, and counted out the money to the exact dollar he knew he had in there. But beside the money in his billfold was something else I recognized: the other half of the little, thin bluish-gray stone he'd given me a month earlier.

I took it out of his billfold and gazed at it between my two fingers, as if it were something that had fallen from space. Neal could have thrown it into his cart and it got mixed in with everything else in there. Instead, he'd kept that rock as safe as his money.

A week later, Neal was back from the hospital, lying on the sidewalk in front of the cemetery in Harvard Square with a twelve pack of Natural Light beer sitting next to him, like man's best friend. In technical terms, Neal had left the hospital against medical advice. In everyday language, he didn't want to stay in the hospital any longer and just got up and left. That day, I faced a moral conundrum that I hadn't felt before: as a true friend, should I take away his beer?

But I didn't. Truth be told, I was just too chicken. I also knew that Neal's decision to stop drinking would have to be his own.

Neal's holiday away from the hospital didn't last long. Amy had just come back from her vacation, and it was just in time to readmit Neal to the hospital.

Back at the hospital the next day, Neal looked like he was doing great, and soon he was transferred to a medical respite care center to recuperate. After a couple of days, though, Neal was back in Harvard Square, after leaving the respite center against medical advice again. Amy came by and told us about her vacation. It was the kind of reunion with Amy we thought we might not ever have.

But three days later, Neal was talking about how lethargic he was because of his new medications. He sat on the bench inside the little glass bus stop on Neal's Island and told me, "I think I'll go back to the medical respite center tomorrow. I'm happy there. I'm too tired out here."

"Yeah, and you don't have any of this there," I said, pointing to his beer. "You don't *have* to have this out here," I reminded him.

I walked across the street to campus, and when I saw him a little while later, Neal made the kind of declaration everyone wants to hear from an alcoholic. "I'm done drinking," he said. "I'm tired of this crap. It's boring."

Hank took Neal's forty-ounce bottle of beer and, with Neal's approval, poured it all out into the street. Was Neal really ending his drinking? Could he stop that easily?

Later that day, I was with Hank when Chubby John texted me that Neal had returned to the hospital. This time, Neal's cart went with him on the ambulance.

The hospital didn't keep him for long, though. Neal returned to Neal's Island in the middle of the night, and by the next morning, he was lethargic and yearning to return to the medical respite center he had recently left.

I called the center and learned the procedure to get him back in.

Neal rested on the ground of Neal's Island, under a crab apple tree where he sometimes relaxed. I watched him as I leaned against the wooden rail fence a few feet away. He ate a bite from a muffin, sat up on a piece of cardboard he was lying on, and picked up a colorful leaf from the ground. He admired it like a botanist.

After a few minutes, Neal tossed his beer can and said, "C'mon,

John," as if he were calling an army into battle. In a way, maybe he was. Maybe he was deciding that now was the time to battle his addiction.

As I took his cart and pulled it in back of me, I realized for the first time just how heavy it was for one person to haul. I followed Neal through Neal's Island, where we had talked about love and marriage, across the street, where he had taught me the art of stemming, and down the sidewalk by CVS, where he had sung songs, goofed off, and smiled at women as if they were as interested in talking to him as he was in talking to them.

As we walked to the other bus stop in Harvard Square, Neal's suit coat fell off the cart, unbeknownst to us. A young man noticed it, though, picked it up, and handed it to me. Walking through the square, I had an unusual sentimental feeling — a sense of finality, like when a soldier leaves for boot camp. In my mind, Neal was moving away. Nothing would be the same. For me, the walk was like Neal's farewell parade, but no one was waving goodbye. No one paid any attention. The only person who noticed was the guy who had picked up Neal's fallen coat, and maybe whoever was stemming outside CVS as we walked by. It seemed no one cared about Neal's decision to leave the streets and his drinking. It seemed no one cared that he was choosing to admit himself to a center with the ability to help him, as long as he had faith that he could be helped. He was leaving behind the only life I'd ever known him to have.

"I'm so weak," Neal said, sitting in the waiting area of the emergency room, awaiting the referral he needed to get back into the medical respite center. "I'm going to die. I can't take it anymore. I hate this. I'm starting to detox." He lifted his arm and showed me how he was getting the shakes. After we sat there for a while, he began feeling worse and laid down on the tiles of the floor. "I'll lay down on the floor. I don't care," he said. In a way, it was a declaration that he didn't care what anyone else might have thought of him, like that evening in Harvard Square when he lay, facedown, on the brick sidewalk.

As time ticked by, Neal began dreaming about the medical respite center — how comfortable it would be and how he was looking forward to returning to it. He wasn't thinking about the restrictions on his lifestyle that caused him to leave it the first time.

"I'm gonna live there," he said. "Forget this. I can't live like this."

"Don't worry about any of us in Harvard Square," I said. "We'll all take care of ourselves."

"I won't be able to see my sunflower," he said, speaking of his prized specimen growing on Neal's Island. Reality was setting in for Neal. "Can you take a picture of it?"

"I don't have a camera. But maybe Amy can," I said.

Neal was concerned about his potted plants and began giving me instructions about them. He told me about the one hanging in a bush by the cemetery and about how he wanted me to put the pots in the ground before winter. "Do some gardening," he said. "It'll be good for you."

After a long wait, a doctor was able to see Neal. Then we waited to learn whether the respite center had any space available for him, since we had heard that it was full.

"Thanks for being my friend, John," Neal said as I stood by his bed.

"Thanks for being my friend," I said.

The good news came that a room was available at the respite center. "Oh, they got me a room!" Neal exclaimed with a sense of joy and relief. He began telling me about the center like a new college student talks about his dorm room. "Wait till you see this place, John."

Telling me about one of the employees, he said, "She comes around every morning and talks to me; sees if there's anything I'd like to do, ya know. It's so nice knowing I'm getting in. Forget that sleeping outside stuff. Especially down here. I don't know the area," he said, referring to inner-city Boston, where he'd considered staying if he needed to wait for a room to become available in the respite center.

"I'll be there for a while," he told me, making sure I knew he'd not be back in Harvard Square soon.

"You might be there for good," I said, not realizing the center provided only temporary assistance. "How do you feel about that?"

Neal didn't like that idea. "Well, I won't be there for too long because I can't go anywhere or do anything except go to the bank and other appointments," he said. He must not have had the same sense of finality walking through Harvard Square that I had had a few hours earlier.

Neal and I walked across the street to the respite center. Because of the center's rules, I wasn't allowed to accompany him to the office where he would be admitted. I walked him to the elevator and we shook hands.

"Take care, bro," I said.

"Thank you, brother."

We waved goodbye as the doors of the elevator closed.

As the yellow daylilies on Neal's Island began to die out for the season, the end of the summer brought a lot of changes in the Harvard Square homeless community. As a way to show appreciation to everyone for accepting me on the streets, I hosted a party in the Common. On the invitations I passed out, I thanked everyone for allowing me to be part of their community and noted that I'd be leaving the streets on August 31, but would be staying in the area for the next school year.

The night before the party, remnants of Tropical Storm Danny ripped through the Boston area, soaking everything in its way, including me, trying to stay dry in the Common. Rain poured all the next day, canceling the party, and all I could hope for was nice weather to return the next day. Thankfully it did. On Sunday afternoon, around thirty people came out for the picnic, including several I didn't know and some I'd never even seen before.

A few days before the party, Hank had taken me to a low-priced grocery store to buy most of the food we'd need for the cookout. Between the two of us, we carried all the food back to the Square, with Hank carrying a case of twenty-four bottles of water on his shoulder like it was a bag of feathers. As we walked, though, I couldn't reach my friend who lived in an apartment in the Square, which meant I didn't have anyplace to store the food.

"We could put it in the cemetery," I suggested to Hank as we walked. That would have been the easiest option, although there was no way to keep the food cool there.

"No, it would all get stolen. It'd all be gone," Hank said, peppering his sentences with curse words, as usual.

"We could stash it in the bushes," I added. But I should have remembered that wasn't a good idea. Earlier in the summer, I had stashed a styrofoam box of leftovers from a restaurant in the cemetery. I carefully hid it, but when I fetched the box a few hours later, a squirrel had chewed a hole in it and eaten all of the tortillas inside. Thankfully, the squirrel didn't eat the rest of the food.

The hardship of keeping groceries without a home hit me like it never had before, now that we were walking with sacks of groceries and had no place to take them. Over the summer, I had some lockers on campus in which I could keep my belongings, such as clothes, books, snack cakes, and my laptop computer. This privilege put me at a huge advantage over others who didn't have any such space for their goods. I also occasionally made use of the sidewalk dispensers that contained free advertising booklets that nobody ever seemed to pay attention to. Besides Hank and me, I had never seen anyone else open them, so we sometimes used them to stash food overnight.

Hank suggested that Graham's apartment, where he stayed, would be the ideal place to take the food for the party. So with Graham's approval, we took it there.

On the day of the party, Hank cooked all of the hotdogs at Graham's place, after which we hauled everything to the Common, like some catering duo. I don't know what I would have done without Hank's help. Together, we served hotdogs, potato chips, potato salad, bottles of punch and water, and seedless watermelon.

Hank served the hotdogs, while I dished out potato salad and distributed chips to each person. As people thanked me for hosting the party, I thanked them for coming. Every last bit of fifty-two dollars' worth of food and drink was consumed.

Raising her bottle of water to the sky, Doris announced that she wanted to make a toast. Looking at me, and then at those around her, she said, "I propose a toast to John, for coming out here to Cambridge and trying to be our friend."

"Trying?" Hank hastily objected. Then he corrected her, "You mean for *being* our friend."

"And for being our friend," Doris continued. "And sleeping out here and spending time with us and helping us. For being part of our community."

A man in the community who'd been homeless for years also made an announcement. "John, I grant you an honorary degree in homelessness."

"From you, that means a lot," I said.

"Well, it's an honorary degree," he added with a smile. "So you've got to act with honor."

Jersey — the one who'd taken away Neal's cart that day when he went to the movie theater — raised her bottle. "You're great, John," she said, followed with a kiss on my cheek and the good news that she was free of warrants after just coming out of twenty-five days in jail.

Doris turned on a pink boom box and played music. Some danced to the beat while others played catch with a sockball — a ball, of sorts, formed by rolling a couple of socks together.

With her cell phone, Doris took a couple of pictures of the group, which included Spare Change Spencer, Chubby John, Jared, George, Charlie, Amy, as well as many others, including the drug dealer who purportedly had stolen Harvard's tents.

Someone on the streets that summer once told me that it was hard for her to think of me as having a life off the streets. In a way, whoever we are or whatever our social conditions may be, all of us have different lives than others may know us to have. Because of the way we sometimes see people, though, we don't always see a person for who she completely is. We're unable to see the entirety of her past, the fragility of her emotions, the uniqueness of her personality, or her hopes for her future. We learn more about each other when we're separated from the stereotypes that could disrupt potential relationships and inflict certain biases. When we're separated from our stereotypes, we're more open with ourselves and people around us. We learn that no one is "the other"; instead, everyone is just like you and me. Despite our perceived and actual differences, down deep, each human soul is somehow connected. We've all felt brokenness in some way, walked down crooked paths in life, and some of us may even have scars from when we've fallen after having lost our way. But we're all redeemable, even if we don't feel like we are.

When we forget stereotypes and seek to know people for who they truly are, we give them a chance. And in return, we give ourselves a chance — to love, flourish, and truly live. It is in that vulnerable place in life — where we are our true selves — that others can bring change within us. And it's in that place that we better understand that though people are different from each other, we're really still the same.

Through ten weeks on the streets, I journeyed with Neal, Dane, George, Chubby John, and our other street companions. I didn't save anyone from the streets. I simply shared in their joys and sorrows, and they shared in mine. I embarked upon new relationships that helped me understand life on the streets a little better, seeing up close and personal what it was like to be homeless at Harvard.

CONCLUSION

On the evening of my last day on the streets, I shook hands with Spare Change Spencer and Doris; we smiled at each other, said some parting words, and I moved into a nearby apartment. Although I had seen the living room and kitchen, I had never seen what would become my bedroom. But little details like how small it was, the shade of the bright blue and red walls, and that it didn't have curtains — until one of my homeless friends offered to hang some for me — didn't matter. The rent was affordable, the location was a good one, the roommates seemed like a great match, and it was indoors.

A couple of hours later, when I was walking through Harvard Square again, Spare Change Spencer shouted to me from a distance, "John, where's your backpack?" With a big grin that erupted into a laugh, he wrapped his arms around me in a giant bear hug, something he excelled at giving. Spencer had always seen my backpack attached to me like a fifth limb, and he was happy I didn't need it any longer.

Spare Change Spencer had been in the process of finding an apartment for himself, and he soon found a place of his own. It was far away, and I think small, but he didn't mind. That night, I invited

Spencer to sleep at my apartment, but when we learned that one of my roommates would also be moving in the same night, Spencer declined, saying, "No, I'll be gettin' up early to sell my papers. So I'll just sleep outside tonight."

Spare Change Spencer and I had had a lot of good times together. He'd gone with me to an orchestra concert on Harvard's campus one night and told me afterward that he'd never been to a concert like that before. Another time, he and two other homeless men joined me for Sunday dinner at my friend's home. When we went around the table, each sharing what we were grateful for, Spencer said that he was thankful for being at that meal. I'd spent hours sitting and talking with Spencer as he sold his papers during the day, and we often slept near each other in the Common.

The night after Tropical Storm Danny assaulted the area with wind and rain, the two of us stayed with Graham and Hank at Graham's apartment. At first, Graham was going to invite just me, but I wasn't going to leave Spencer, so he was invited too, although Hank bought Graham a sandwich to sweeten the deal. Even though he never could remember my name, Graham enjoyed the extra company that night, saying, "You're my brother, both of ya's."

"Yeah," I said. "Street brothers."

That was first time I'd slept indoors in nearly ten weeks. Graham's offer was too good to pass up, because my sleeping bag was sopping wet after the storm the previous night. I'd left it, the abandoned tent, and some of my clothes — soaked as they were — in the Common all day and the next night, when we were sleeping on Graham's floor. When I went back the next day, my sleeping bag and the tent were gone. I never saw them again.

Despite the differences among those in our community, commonalities drew us together. We all had good days and bad days. We shared our problems with each other. My homeless friends took an interest in me, listened to me, and talked with me, helping and supporting me when I was in need. We enjoyed eating together and sharing food with each other. Some of my homeless friends enjoyed teasing me about how long I saved leftovers in my backpack — far longer than some would think is reasonable.

That summer helped me think about life from a new perspective. Seeing people sleep outside every night can't help but remind you how vulnerable we are as human beings. And there was the time some of us went with our non-homeless friend Joe in his car for an evening drive. We drove out into the country, which smelled of freshly cut grass, and into a little town, where Joe had planned to take us to get ice cream. Spare Change Spencer told us that night that he hadn't had ice cream in two years, reminding me just how fortunate I have been to enjoy life's little luxuries.

The summer had nearly ended, and over the next few weeks and months, for some in the homeless community, life was different; for others, it probably seemed the same. Life was changing for everyone, though, because in big or small ways, that's what it always does.

Joining my family and me at my graduation that next May were Chubby John, Spare Change Spencer, Charlie, and Bob. I was honored that they came to support me, and we took pictures outside the Memorial Church in Harvard Yard.

As for Dane, after coming out of the hospital, he got a room in a rooming house and keeps in touch with his two adult children, continues playing music, and speaks occasionally at events about his homeless experiences.

George found temporary housing, began working with the local

American Legion, and continues spending time with his friends on the streets.

After being housed, Chubby John participated in raising money for a charity walk organized by Starlight Ministries. It was his way of giving back to a charity that, with its team of volunteers, had shared food and social support each week with the homeless community. Chubby John seemed to always appreciate opportunities to be a voice for the homeless, and I invited him to be a guest speaker for a class at Harvard that next semester. He was also invited to participate as a panel member for a discussion forum about homelessness at a local church in an effort to bring about better awareness of how to best serve those on the streets.

As for Neal, eight days after I said goodbye to him at the medical respite center, Spare Change Spencer texted me that he was back in Harvard Square. I saw him sleeping in the Coop, with a new cart beside him.

Seeing Neal out of the medical respite center reminded me of something I had thought about over the summer. One of the phenomena I'd thought I'd noticed was just how addictive the homeless lifestyle — for some — seemed to be. However, upon further reflection, rather than believing that homelessness in and of itself is compelling, I now think it's more accurate to say that there are aspects of street life that grip some people, just like George had talked about the streets grabbing him. The fierce undercurrent of things like alcohol, friends, or drugs can all suck people back onto the streets before they even leave. Complicating this are conditions that many people on the streets face, such as mental illness or developmental disabilities, emotional fragility, spiritual despair, unemployment, lack of social safety nets, or a personal resolution that being down and out is part of who they are. Some people's actions and words were probably a result of what was going on inside of their minds or bodies that they may not have been able to completely control. That summer, I don't think I ever came to a full realization of that.

The next day, Neal said he was tired of people telling him not to drink. He just wanted people to accept him and his decisions. While he said he was committed to drinking less, he said something that powerfully summed up how he understood his life. "People shouldn't assume I was on the right track by going back to the center, because I never have been on the right track, and I never will."

I told Neal that people loved and cared about him, and that's why people were concerned. But Neal just replied, "Homeless people have their own problems and shouldn't be telling me what to do."

A few days later, Neal, sporting a new haircut, was selling some of his knickknacks, which were spread out on a cloth on the sidewalk in front of the cemetery. He sat beside his items, which included wooden boxes, a cardboard animal-cracker box, and binoculars. "If it sells, fine. If it doesn't, fine. I don't care," he said. Selling his items that day, Neal told me that every morning he raises his hands up and stretches them toward heaven and says, "Lord, your will be done."

Soon, I'd hear a report that Neal had returned to his mother's home for a little while and was driving her car. Neal was free to live with his mother, but street life kept beckoning him — to warm places in the winter and, in the summer, to Harvard Square, or somewhere not far away.

So here it was, the end of my last day on the streets. I hugged Spare Change Spencer goodbye for the second time that night, said goodnight, collected my belongings from Neal's Island, and walked to my new apartment. After the summer was over, I continued to see

Spencer, as well as others from the community, in the Square, in my apartment, or where they lived.

My buddy, Josh, had helped me move a few boxes of personal items into my apartment, and it was time to clean up and settle in. I fried up two big hamburgers on the stove and cleaned the wooden floor of my bedroom, as well as the mattress that lay on it, without a frame, that someone next door had given to me. Its previous owner had finished school and was leaving town. My bedroom wasn't all that was in need of cleaning, however, and I squirted Clorox Clean-Up Cleaner with Bleach on my feet and toes and took a shower. I then put sheets on the mattress, and when I laid down on it, I noticed how soft it was compared with the ground. I thought that night about a formerly homeless man somebody had told me about who, after moving into an apartment, just slept on the floor. I guess after so many years of being homeless, his mattress felt too soft.

For many people's standards, my apartment was far from perfect. The kitchen still had food on the shelves from past tenants, although, of course, that didn't bother me. The old brown La-Z-Boy in the kitchen — also left by previous tenants — sat so close to the wall it could never be reclined. But I still liked it. None of the apartment's deficiencies bothered me. Just like Dane had said, "You'll really appreciate inside life more now, having been out here."

I was content. I was home.